North Coast and Cascades Network Climate Monitoring Report

North Cascades National Park Complex; Water Year 2010

Natural Resource Data Series NPS/NCCN/NRDS—2012/261

Michael Larrabee

National Park Service
North Coast and Cascades Network
North Cascades National Park Complex
810 State Route 20
Sedro-Woolley, WA 98284

Bill Baccus

National Park Service
North Coast and Cascades Network
Olympic National Park
600 East Park Avenue
Port Angeles, WA 98362

Rebecca Lofgren and Mark Huff

National Park Service
North Coast and Cascades Network
Mount Rainier National Park
55210 238th Ave E.
Ashford, WA 98304

March 2012

U.S. Department of the Interior
National Park Service
Natural Resource Stewardship and Science
Fort Collins, Colorado

The National Park Service, Natural Resource Stewardship and Science office in Fort Collins, Colorado publishes a range of reports that address natural resource topics of interest and applicability to a broad audience in the National Park Service and others in natural resource management, including scientists, conservation and environmental constituencies, and the public.

The Natural Resource Data Series is intended for the timely release of basic data sets and data summaries. Care has been taken to assure accuracy of raw data values, but a thorough analysis and interpretation of the data has not been completed. Consequently, the initial analyses of data in this report are provisional and subject to change.

All manuscripts in the series receive the appropriate level of peer review to ensure that the information is scientifically credible, technically accurate, appropriately written for the intended audience, and designed and published in a professional manner. This report received informal peer review by subject-matter experts who were not directly involved in the collection, analysis, or reporting of the data. Data in this report were collected and analyzed using methods based on established, peer-reviewed protocols and were analyzed and interpreted within the guidelines of the protocols.

Views, statements, findings, conclusions, recommendations, and data in this report do not necessarily reflect views and policies of the National Park Service, U.S. Department of the Interior. Mention of trade names or commercial products does not constitute endorsement or recommendation for use by the U.S. Government.

This report is available from The North Coast and Cascades Network Inventory and Monitoring website (http://science.nature.nps.gov/im/units/nccn/reportpubs.cfm) and the Natural Resource Publications Management website (http://www.nature.nps.gov/publications/nrpm/).

Please cite this publication as:

Larrabee, M. A., B. Baccus, R. Lofgren, and M. Huff. 2011. North Coast and Cascades Network climate monitoring report: North Cascades National Park Complex; water year 2010. Natural Resource Data Series NPS/NCCN/NRDS—2012/261. National Park Service, Fort Collins, Colorado.

NPS 963/113088, March 2012

Contents

Figures

Figures (continued)

Figures (continued)

Tables

Appendices

Executive Summary

Climate and weather events define many of the abiotic features of habitat found in national parks and are key to understanding and interpreting changes in natural resources. Everyday park operations including; fire management, search and rescue, maintenance of park infrastructure, and visitor use are influenced by weather. Monitoring weather and maintaining climate records provides essential information to support park operations and monitor park resources.

This report summarizes climate data collected in the North Cascades National Park Complex for Water Year 2010, and is part of a set of climate summary reports from seven national and historic parks in the North Coast and Cascades Network. Published in the National Park Service's Natural Resource Data Series, annual climate summary reports are intended to provide basic data sets and data summaries in a timely manner, with minimal interpretation and analyses. We envision National Park staff, especially, planners, scientists, interpreters, partners; and interested public as the primary audience for these reports.

Temperature and precipitation data are presented from six weather stations. These stations are located on both western and eastern slopes of the North Cascades Range at both low and high elevation sites. Data were recorded using automated instruments operated by the National Park Service and other collaborators, including the National Weather Service (NWS) and the Natural Resources Conservation Service (NRCS). For two stations with long term records, the Ross Dam Cooperative Observer (COOP) station on the west side of the Cascade crest and the Stehekin COOP on the drier, east side of the park, monthly average temperatures and monthly total precipitation are reported and compared to the 30-year normal. Monthly snow depth and snow water equivalent are reported for one Snow Telemetry (SNOTEL) site and two NWS COOP stations within the park. Two NPS GLACIER climate stations provide air temperature at high elevations in alpine environments. A NWS US Climate Reference Network (USCRN) station located in Marblemount represents lowland areas on the west slopes of the North Cascade Range. A series of appendices present daily and monthly air temperature, precipitation and snowpack data from six park operated weather stations, including comparisons to period of record and highlights of important weather events from each site.

In summary, average annual temperatures and precipitation were both near normal for Water Year 2010; however significant monthly departures for both parameters were documented. Overall, conditions in winter were warm and dry, with a shift to cooler and wetter conditions in the spring through early summer. Snowpack remained below normal during the warmer, drier winter months only to recover to above normal due to a wetter, cooler late spring that persisted into late June.

Acknowledgments

North Cascades National Park Complex relies on several cooperating agencies to help support and maintain a long-term climate monitoring program as part of the North Coast and Cascades (NCCN) climate monitoring program. These agencies include:

- National Weather Service – National Weather Service Cooperative Observer Program

- Natural Resources & Conservation Service - National Water and Climate Center, SNOTEL and Snow Survey Program

- US Climate Reference Network, National Oceanic and Atmospheric Administration – National Climate Data Center.

- National Interagency Fire Center – Remote Automated Weather Stations Program

Data management is critical to provide for the availability and analysis of climate data. We depend on the NCCN Data Managers, specifically John Boetsch and Bret Christoe; the Western Regional Climate Center; and the National Climate Data Center for climate data management.

The authors appreciate the careful review by Catharine Copass and Jon Riedel. Finally, we thank the Office of the Washington State Climatologist and Dr. Cliff Mass (Weather Blog) for their regional and statewide weather and climate summaries.

.

Acronyms

COOP	Cooperative Observer Station
I&M	Inventory and Monitoring
NCCN	North Coast and Cascades Network
NCDC	National Climatic Data Center
NPS	National Park Service
NOAA	National Oceanic and Atmospheric Administration
NOCA	North Cascades National Park Service Complex
NRCS	Natural Resources Conservation Service
NWS	National Weather Service
PNW	Pacific Northwest
RAWS	Remote Automated Weather Stations
SNOTEL	Snowpack Telemetry
SWE	Snow Water Equivalent
USCRN	United States Climate Reference Network
USDA	United States Department of Agriculture
WRCC	Western Regional Climate Center

Glossary

Climate Normals: A long-term average value of a meteorological parameter (i.e. temperature) for a certain area. For example, "temperatures are normal for this time of year" means that temperatures are at or near the average climatological value for a given time period. Climate normals are usually taken from data averaged over a 30-year period (e.g., 1971-2000 average), and are concerned with the distribution of data within limits of common occurrence.

Fall: The National Weather Service defines fall as the months of September, October and November.

NWS-COOP: An extensive network of manually operated weather stations overseen by the National Weather Service. Many Cooperative Observer Program weather sites were established in the late 1800's and as such, provide the best long term data sites for understanding local climates. At each station, an observer records daily maximum and minimum temperature, as well as total rain and snowfall.

NPS-GLACIER: A network of two climate stations operated by the National Park Service. The stations are located at high elevation sites, adjacent to Silver Glacier and Noisy Creek Glacier, two index glaciers monitored by the NPS. Meteorological parameters measured at each site include temperature, relative humidity, wind speed and direction and net solar radiation.

Period of Record: The total span of time that climate data have been collected at a specific location. The longer the period of record, the more likely the climate data will not be biased by singular weather events or cyclic climate anomalies such as those associated with the Pacific Decadal Oscillation.

RAWS: A network of remote automated weather stations that provide real-time weather data to assist land management agencies in monitoring fuels, rating fire danger and predicting fire behavior. RAWS stations are all operational during summer months, but many at lower elevations operate on a year round basis.

SNOTEL: An automated network of snowpack data collection sites operated by the Natural Resources Conservation Service (NRCS). A standard SNOTEL site consists of a snow pillow, snow depth sensor, a storage type precipitation gage and air temperature sensor. Enhanced sites also measure soil moisture.

Snow Course: A site where trained observers manually measure snow depth, water equivalent and density at a series of points along an established transect. Measurements are taken the last week of each month during winter and early spring. Values are recorded as the first of the month.

Snow Water Equivalent (SWE): A measurement describing the amount of water contained within the seasonal snowpack. It can be thought of as the depth of water that would theoretically result if you melted the entire snowpack instantaneously.

Spring: The National Weather Service defines spring as the months of March, April and May.

Summer: The National Weather Service defines summer as the months of June, July, and August.

Water Year: The Water Year (or Hydrologic Year) is most often defined as the period from October 1st to September 30 of the following year. It is called by the calendar year in which it ends. Thus, Water Year 2010 is the 12-month period beginning October 1, 2009 and ending September 30, 2010. The period is chosen so as to encompass a full cycle of precipitation accumulation.

Winter: The National Weather Service defines winter as the months of December, January and February.

Introduction

Climate is a dominant driver of the physical and ecologic processes of the North Coast and Cascades Inventory and Monitoring Network (NCCN) (Davey et al. 2006). Trends in precipitation and temperature influence how an ecosystem and its organisms function. The quantity and timing of rainfall and snow can influence the productivity and health of forests (Nakawatase and Peterson 2006), the amount of water flowing in streams and rivers (Hamlet et al. 2007) and the growing or shrinking of mountain glaciers. Likewise, temperature can influence the quantity and timing of plant growth and stream runoff, or the extent and duration of winter snowpack and lake ice. (Thompson et al. 2009). Through direct and indirect methods, climate affects the behavior and reproduction of terrestrial and aquatic animal species (Crozier et al. 2008). Climate is one of the primary causes of disturbance events such as forest fires (Littell and Gwozdz 2011), avalanches, windstorms and floods. These events can have a major impact on park landscapes and their associated ecosystems.

Given the importance of climate, it has been identified as a primary vital sign by all 32 Inventory and Monitoring (I&M) networks within the NPS (Gray 2008). The NCCN (Figure 1) monitors climate in order to: understand variations in other park resources being monitored; compare current and historic data to understand long-term trends; and to provide data for modeling impacts to park facilities and resources in the future (Lofgren et al. 2010). Climate data, derived from the NCCN climate network will play an important role in understanding and interpreting the physical and ecological Vital Signs monitored by I&M within NCCN parks.

The NCCN climate monitoring program capitalizes on climate stations operated by partnering agencies. The NCCN climate monitoring program compiles data from over 60 weather stations in and adjacent to the parks, 15 of which are operated by the National Park Service. While a wide variety of climate parameters are measured as part of the NCCN climate program, this report focuses on two key parameters: precipitation and air temperature, while providing supplemental information on snowpack.

This report summarizes climate data collected from six weather stations located in and adjacent to the North Cascades National Park Complex during the 2010 water year, and is part of a set of climate summary reports from seven national and historic parks in the NCCN. Temperature, precipitation, and snow data from the six weather stations are summarized in the Results section of this report. Additional climate data recorded from each weather station are presented in Appendices A through E.

Annual climate summary reports are intended to provide basic data sets and data summaries in a timely manner, with minimal interpretation and analyses. National Park staff, planners, scientists, interpreters, partners; and interested public are the primary audience.

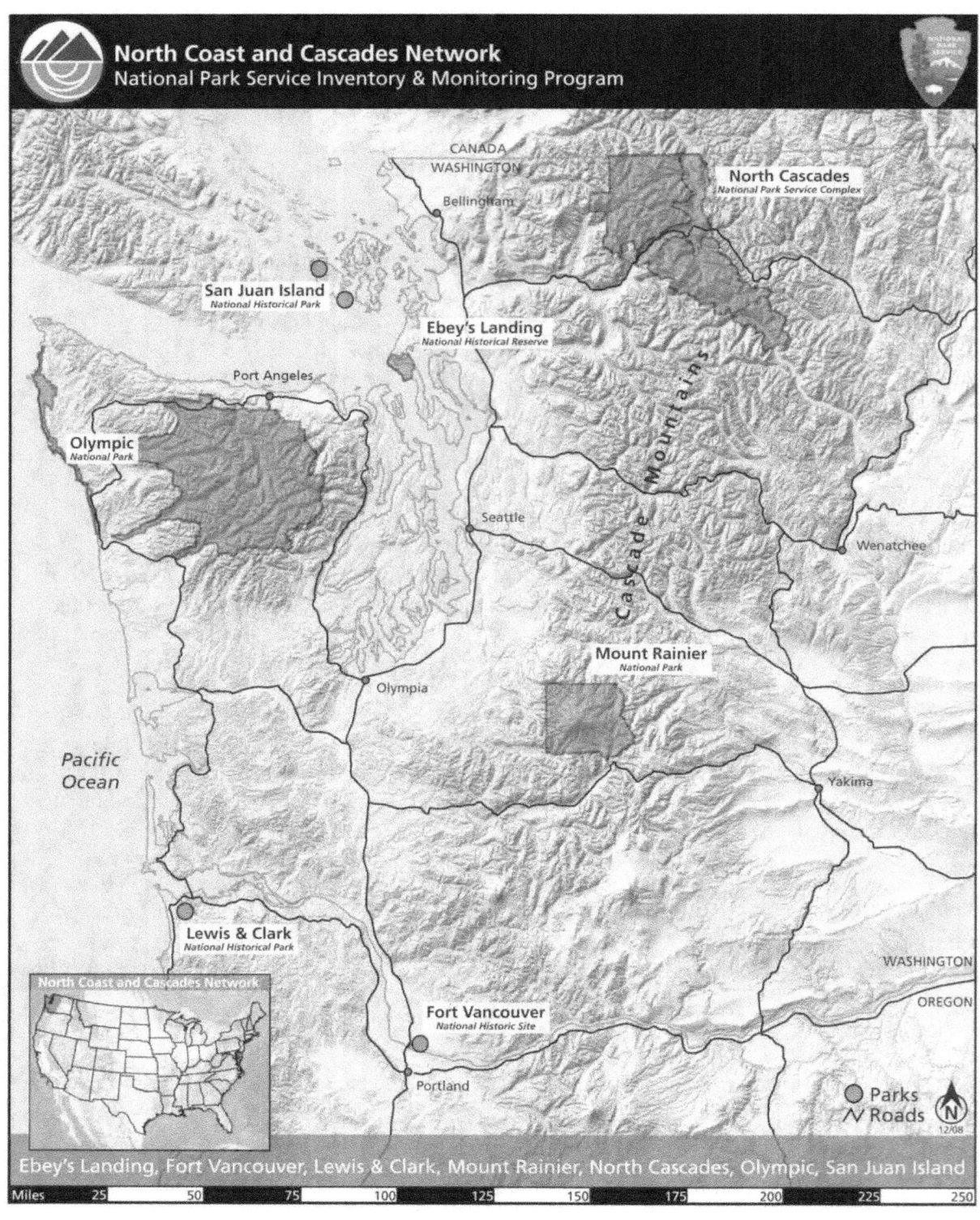

Figure 1. North Coast and Cascades Network (NCCN).

Methods

Station Locations

This report incorporates data collected from weather stations operated by the NPS (GLACIER), the Natural Resources Conservation Service (SNOTEL), and the National Weather Service (COOP and USCRN) (Table 1 and Figure 2).

Table 1. Weather stations referenced in this report.

Station Name	Station Type	Location	Elevation (ft)	Forest Zone	Period of Record
Marblemount (Darrington 21 NNE)	USCRN	West	407	Forest	2003 to Present
Noisy Creek	GLACIER	West	6590	Alpine	2009 to Present
Park Creek Ridge	SNOTEL	East	4600	Subalpine	1979 to Present
Ross Dam	COOP	Interior	1240	Forest	1963 to Present
Silver Lake	GLACIER	Interior	7670	Alpine	2009 to Present
Stehekin	COOP	East	1270	Forest	1931 to Present

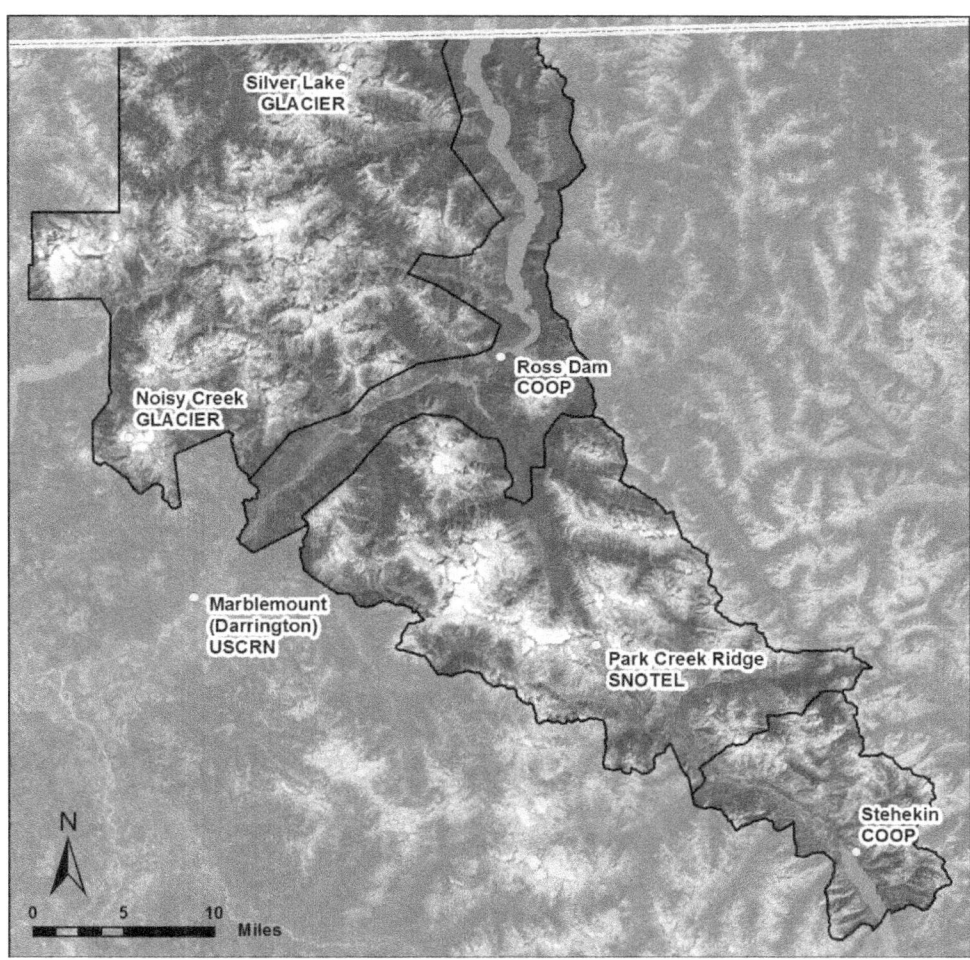

Figure 2. Location of weather stations referenced in this report.

Weather Station Measurements

Weather stations within the NCCN are managed by a variety of different agencies, each with a specific purpose. For this reason, instrumentation, method and period of collection may vary between sites. Table 2 describes the parameters measured at each station, highlights the data which are presented in this report, and indicates which data are available by request from North Cascades National Park Complex.

Table 2. Parameters measured at weather stations included in this report. X indicates that the parameter is measured and data are presented in this report; X indicates parameter is measured and data are available on request.

Station Name	Managing Agency – Station Type	Air Temp	Rh	Precipitation	Snow Depth	Snowfall	Snow Water Equivalent	Net Radiation	Wind Speed & Direction	Soil Temperature	Soil Moisture
Marblemount (Darrington 21NNE)	NWS - USCRN[1]	X	X	X					X		
Noisy Creek	NPS - GLACIER[2]	X	X					X	X		
Park Creek Ridge	NRCS - SNOTEL[3]	X	X	X	X		X		X	X	X
Ross Dam	NWS - COOP[4]	X		X	X	X					
Silver Lake	NPS - GLACIER[2]	X	X					X	X		
Stehekin	NWS - COOP[4]	X		X	X	X					

[1] NWS-USCRN utilize a standard array of automated weather instruments. Parameters are measured every 5 minutes and output as hourly averages.

[2] NPS-GLACIER stations utilize a standard array of automated weather instruments which are measured at 60 second intervals and output as hourly averages. A single snow water equivalent measurement is taken at these sites as part of the long term glacier monitoring program.

[3] NRCS-SNOTEL utilize a standard array of automated weather instruments in support of water supply forecasting. Parameters are measured every 60 seconds, and output as hourly averages.

[4] NWS-COOP stations rely on a standard array of manually operated weather instruments. Parameters are measured and recorded daily.

Data Quality

The Noisy Creek GLACIER weather station temperature data did not meet quality assurance standards and were removed for the entire water year. The problem was linked to poor grounding of the instrument tower. Improvements to tower grounding were performed in Water Year 2011.

The Stehekin COOP weather station is missing all data for September 2010. The cause of the missing data is unknown. For this report, missing temperature and precipitation data for the Stehekin COOP has been replaced with data from the adjacent Stehekin RAWS station.

Data Management

NWS COOP station and NRCS SNOTEL station data used in this report are acquired directly from the managing agencies. Quality assurance and control is provided by these agencies and is described in the NCCN Climate Monitoring Protocol (Lofgren et al. 2010).

The daily data used in this report from NPS and RAWS stations are derived from hourly data which have been evaluated through automated queries and manual display and graphing. Hourly data flagged or identified as suspect are omitted from daily summaries. If more than two hours of data are missing on a given day, no daily values are presented.

Monthly values are generated and presented for stations where five or fewer daily values are missing. In the case of missing precipitation values, daily quantities may be substituted from another nearby weather station for the purposes of reporting monthly and annual totals. This will only occur when nearby data are available and a known correlation exists between these sites. In these cases where estimates are generated from nearby stations, data are footnoted and a description of the quantity and source of data replacement is given.

Data Reporting

Data in this report are based on the hydrologic or water year (October 1 to September 30) and organized by month and seasons. Ecosystems in the Pacific Northwest are dominated by two distinct hydrological periods, a wet season generally beginning in late October and ending in June, and a drought season which extends from July to September. While a calendar year divides the wet winter season, the use of a water year closely reflects the timing and seasonality of many physical and ecological processes that are driven by climate, such as soil saturation and forest evapotranspiration, onset and breakup of lake ice, glacial accumulation and ablation balances, magnitude and timing of stream flow, emergence and flowering of plants and migratory timing of bird species.

Seasons in this report are distinguished based on National Weather Service (NWS) standards for the Northern Hemisphere. The NWS defines December, January, and February as winter; March, April, and May as spring; June, July, and August as summer; and September, October, and November as fall.

The main report provides monthly averages of daily average temperatures and monthly total precipitation for all stations listed in Table 2. While routinely collected in metric units, the data are presented in Fahrenheit and inches to facilitate use and interpretation by the public and park staff. Two stations with long term records, Ross Dam and Stehekin are compared to the 30-year climate normal. Snow water equivalent is reported and compared to the 30-year climate normal for one SNOTEL within the park.

The 2010 weather data for each climate station is reported in a separate appendix. Each appendix includes daily precipitation and temperature data. Maximum and minimum temperatures for each month are reported. Daily or monthly snowfall or snow water equivalent is presented when available. Water Year 2010 is compared with the 30-year climate normal in the main report. The appendices feature a comparison of 2010 with the period of record for that station. Detailed discussion of maintenance issues or data concerns associated with each specific station are also presented.

Results

Temperature

For Water Year 2010, the mean annual temperatures were slightly above normal on the west side of the Cascade Crest and slightly below normal on the east side. Ross Dam was 48.9° F, 0.4° above normal (Table 3). Annual temperature at Stehekin was 48° F, 0.2° below normal (Table 3).

The average winter season temperatures were significantly warmer than normal on west and east sides of the Cascade Crest (+2.4° and +2.7°, respectively). Departures from normal for mean monthly temperatures were also greatest during the winter season (Figure 3). The greatest negative departure occurred in December, when temperatures were 2.8° and 3.3° F below normal at the Ross Dam and Stehekin COOP stations, respectively (Figure 3 and 4). This was followed by the greatest positive departure in January, when temperatures were 5.3° and 3.4° F above normal. February was also much warmer than normal, with temperatures 4.7° and 2.6° F above normal (Figures 3 and 5).

At the end of March, a marked shift to a cooler and wetter weather pattern began, and this continued through June, with temperature departures at Ross Dam and Stehekin ranging from 0.8° to 3.1° F below normal (Figure 3). The months of July and August returned to slightly above normal temperatures on the east side (+0.6° F at Stehekin; Figure 4), however west side, low elevation stations, such as Marblemount, reported below average temperatures for these months (-2.4° F; Figure A-1). September temperatures on both sides of the crest were well below normal (-1.4° and -1.3° F at Ross Dam and Stehekin respectively; Figures 3 and 4).

Daily extreme low temperatures were recorded during a prolonged cold period between December 7 and 14, 2009. An absolute low of -8.0° F was recorded on December 8 at the Silver Lake GLACIER (Table D-1). On this same day, low temperatures at Marblemount and Stehekin were 11.1° and 8.0° F respectively (Tables A-1 and E-1). A daily high temperature of 97° F was recorded on July 10 at Stehekin (Table E-1). West side sites recorded the high daily temperatures on August 15, with 98.4° F recorded at Marblemount (Table A-1).

Table 3. Average monthly air temperatures (°F) from weather stations within or adjacent to North Cascades National Park Complex in Water Year 2010.

Season	Month & Year	Marblemount USCRN	Noisy Creek GLACIER	Park Creek Ridge SNOTEL	Ross Dam COOP	Silver Lake GLACIER	Stehekin COOP
Fall	October 2009	47.8	----[a]	37.9	48.1	33.7	45.1
	November 2009	41.4	----[a]	31.2	40.0	29.2	36.8
Winter	December 2009	33.2	----[a]	16.5	31.1	24.2	25.8
	January 2010	42.1	----[a]	28.5	38.4	31.3	32.2
	February 2010	42.9	----[a]	31.3	40.6	29.5	35.1
Spring	March 2010	43.2	----[a]	33.3	42.7	29.0	41.1
	April 2010	46.4	----[a]	35.9	45.9	30.5	46.5
	May 2010	50.7	----[a]	40.6	51.7	36.4	52.9
Summer	June 2010	56.5	----[a]	47.5	57.7	43.6	61.4
	July 2010	63.0	----[a]	57.7	66.4	55.4	70.6
	August 2010	62.8	----[a]	56.5	66.2	53.1	68.3
Fall	September 2010	57.6	----[a]	48.7	58.1	45.7	58.2[b]
Water Year		**49.0**	----[a]	**38.8**	**48.9**	**36.8**	**47.8**

[a] The Noisy Creek GLACIER station temperature data were identified as suspect and removed for entire water year.

[b] The Stehekin COOP station is missing all data for September 2010. For this report, missing temperature and precipitation data for the Stehekin COOP has been replaced with data from the nearby Stehekin RAWS station.

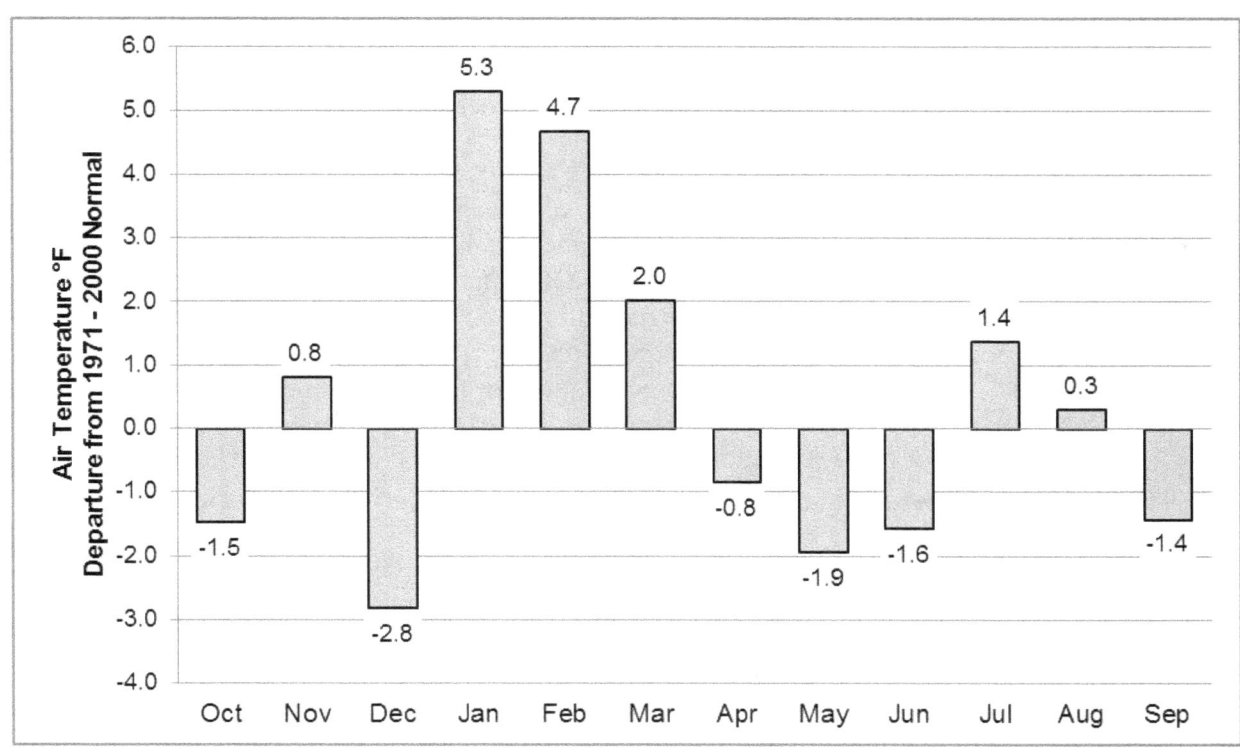

Figure 3. Departure of average monthly temperature (°F) for Ross Dam COOP in Water Year 2010 from monthly averages for the climatological normal 1971-2000.

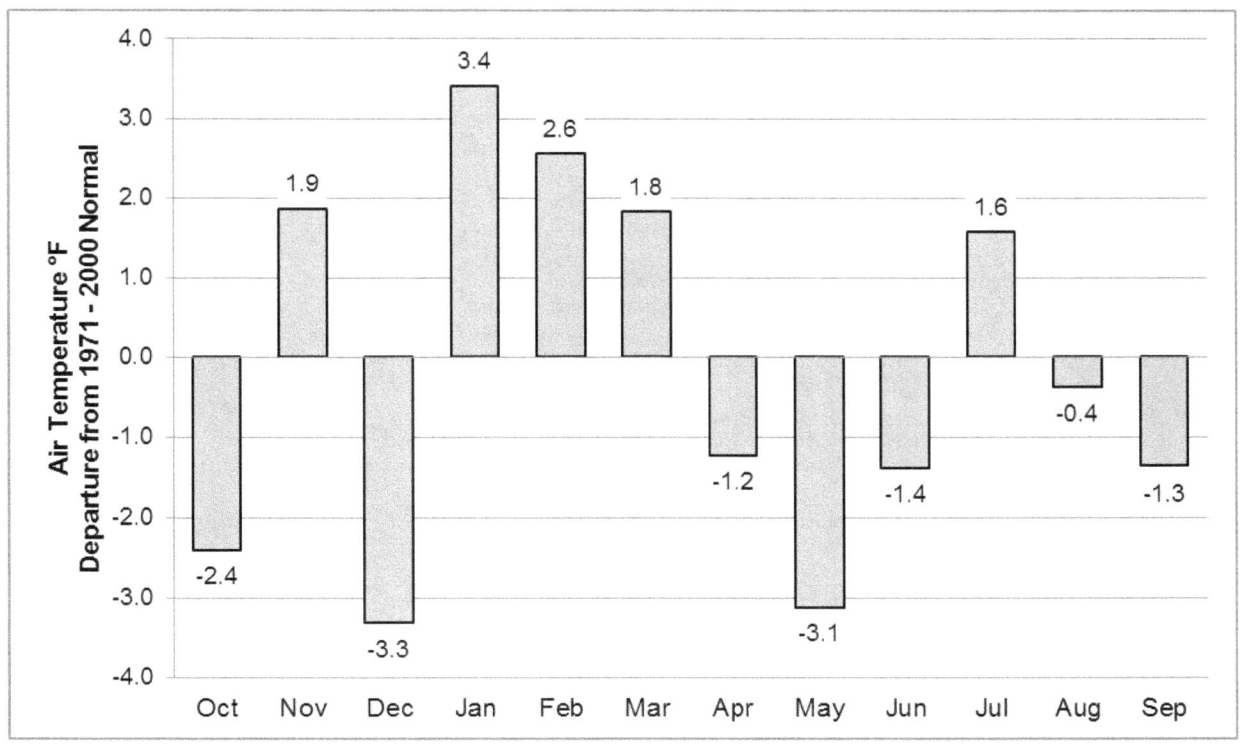

Figure 4. Departure of average monthly temperature (°F) for Stehekin COOP in Water Year 2010 from monthly averages for the climatological normal 1971-2000.

Precipitation

Annual precipitation was normal on the west side of the Cascade Crest and slightly below average on the east side. Ross Dam received 58.5 inches, 101 percent of normal. Stehekin received 33.0 inches, 92 percent of normal (Table 4).

The months of October and November were wetter than normal at Ross Dam and Stehekin (151% and 149% respectively; Figures 5 and 6). November, with 13.9 inches of rainfall, was the seventh wettest November on record at the Ross Dam COOP station, since 1960. Winter months were drier than normal (48% and 60% at Ross Dam and Stehekin respectively) followed by a wetter than normal spring and early summer (Figures 5 and 6). Spring and early summer, from March to June, recorded 141 percent of normal precipitation for those combined months at both Ross Dam and Stehekin (Figures 5 and 6). The month of May exhibited the greatest departure, receiving 191 and 196 percent more precipitation than normal at Ross Dam and Stehekin respectively (Figures 5 and 6).

The late summer months of July and August were generally drier than normal at Ross Dam (69% of normal) and much drier than normal at Stehekin (16% of normal; Figures 5 and 6). July was extremely dry, and three of the four stations had monthly precipitation totals of 0.1 inches or less (Appendices A to E). September brought the return of wetter than normal conditions. During this month, Ross Dam rainfall was 251 percent of normal, while Stehekin received 150 percent of normal precipitation (Figures 5 and 6). At the Park Creek Ridge SNOTEL, September 2010 was the fourth wettest September in 32 years of data collection.

The wettest dates of the year occurred between November 15 to 26, 2009 when Marblemount received 10.9 inches (Figure A-5) and Stehekin received 4.7 inches of precipitation (Figure E-5). The highest daily precipitation was recorded on November 16 at Marblemount (2.5 inches) and November 17 at Stehekin (1.4 inches; Figures A-5 and E-5). At Stehekin, a prolonged period with no precipitation was recorded between June 22 and July 20, a period of 29 days (Figure E-5).

Table 4. Total monthly precipitation (inches) from weather stations within or adjacent to NOCA in Water Year 2010.

Season	Month & Year	Marblemount USCRN	Park Creek Ridge SNOTEL	Ross Dam COOP	Stehekin COOP
Fall	October 2009	14.1	9.2	9.3	5.9
	November 2009	17.7	15.5	13.9	7.0
Winter	December 2009	5.5	4.5	4.2	2.3
	January 2010	8.7	10.7	6.2	6.5
	February 2010	3.3	4.1	1.9	1.8
Spring	March 2010	6.4	5.1	5.2	1.8
	April 2010	4.6	3.8	3.3	2.5
	May 2010	5.7	3.5	4.3	2.0
Summer	June 2010	3.3	2.7	2.8	1.2
	July 2010	0.1	0.1	0.4	0.0
	August 2010	2.6	2.0	1.4	0.2
Fall	September 2010	8.1	4.5	5.7	1.7[a]
Water Year 2010		**80.0**	**65.7**	**58.5**	**33.0[a]**

[a] The Stehekin COOP station is missing all data for September 2010. For this report, missing temperature and precipitation data for the Stehekin COOP has been replaced with data from the nearby Stehekin RAWS station.

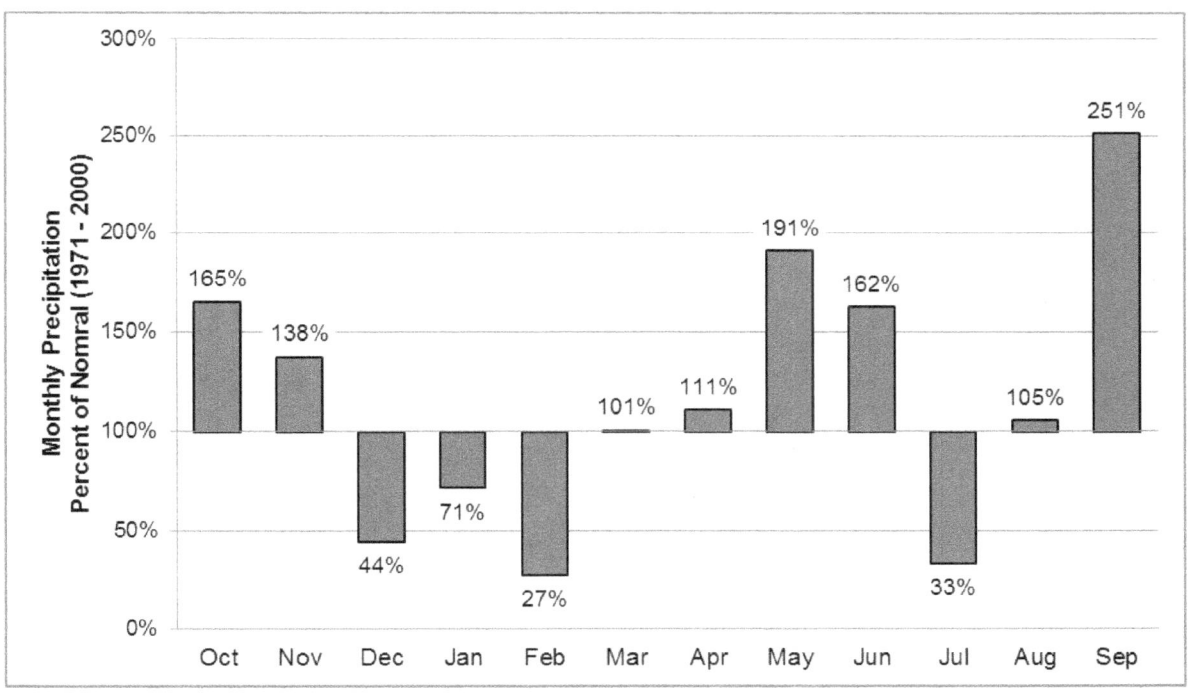

Figure 5. Comparison of total monthly precipitation (inches) at Ross Dam COOP in Water Year 2010 against the climatological normal 1971-2000.

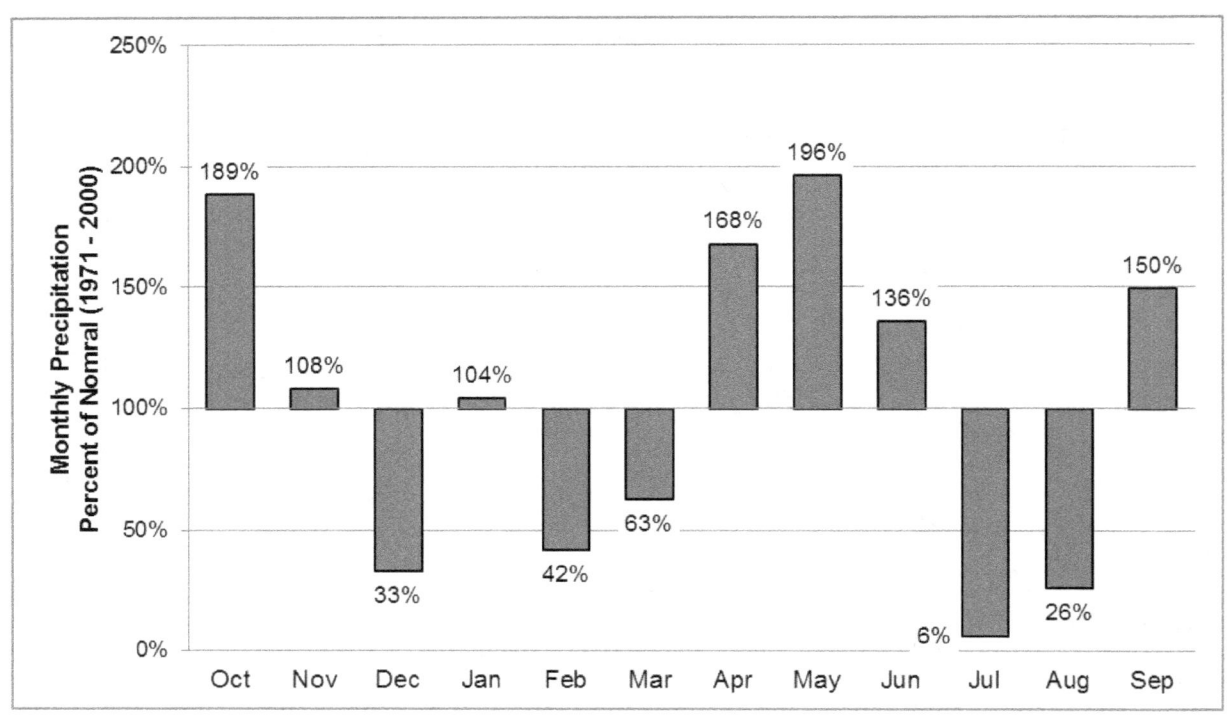

Figure 6. Comparison of total monthly precipitation (inches) at Stehekin COOP in Water Year 2010 against the climatological normal 1971-2000.

Snow

The winter snowpack was slightly below normal in 2010. Snow water equivalent on December 1, 2009 was 77 percent of normal and despite unusually dry conditions from December through March, the snowpack had climbed slightly to 86 percent (Figure 7) by April 1. Significant new snow and colder than normal temperatures for the remainder of spring helped to supplement and preserve the existing snowpack and by June 1, snow water equivalent was well above normal (125%) at the Park Creek Ridge SNOTEL (Figure 7).

Table 5. Snow depth (inches) measured on the first of the month at SNOTEL and snow courses within NOCA during Water Year 2010.

Month & Year	Ross Dam COOP	Park Creek Ridge SNOTEL	Stehekin COOP
November 1st 2009	0.0	0.0	0.0
December 1st 2009	0.0	49.0	5.0
January 1st 2010	2.0	66.0	46.0
February 1st 2010	0.0	90.0	64.0
March 1st 2010	0.0	88.0	35.0
April 1st 2010	0.0	90.0	14.0
May 1st 2010	0.0	66.0	0.0
June 1st 2010	0.0	24.0	0.0
July 1st 2010	0.0	0.0	0.0

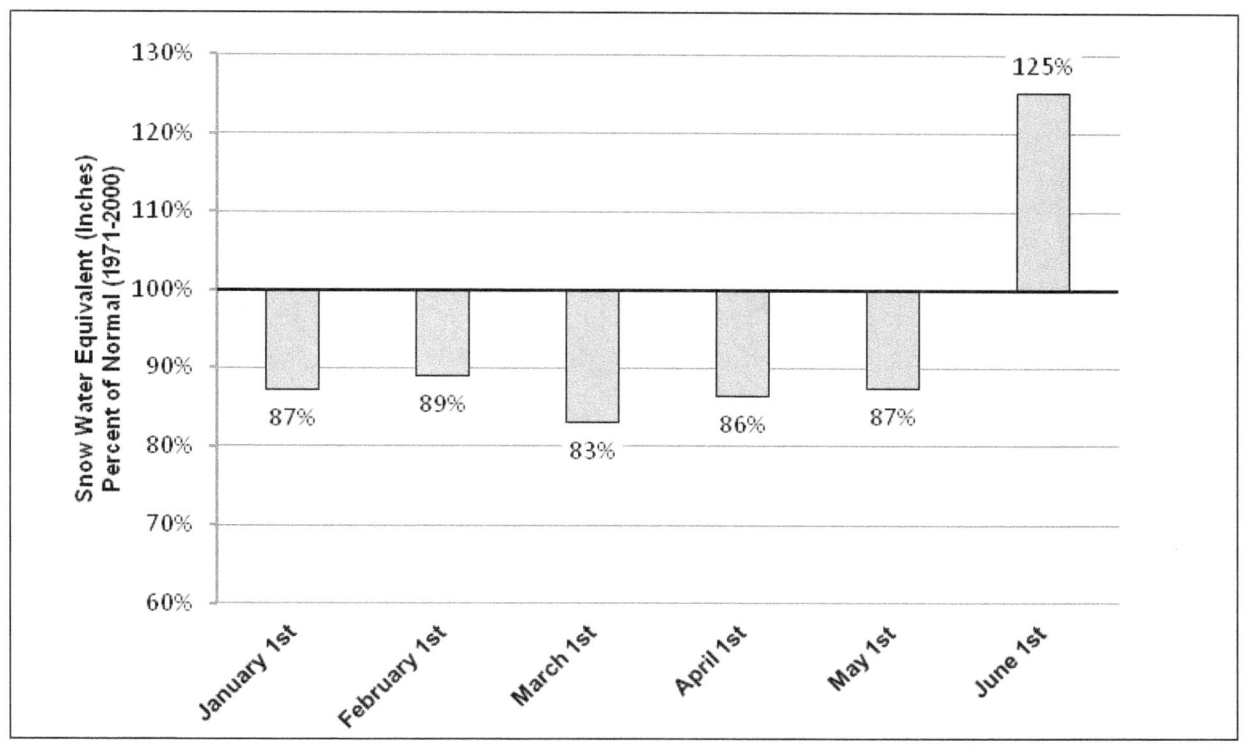

Figure 7. Comparison of snow water equivalent (inches) at the Park Creek Ridge SNOTEL in Water Year 2010 against the climatological normal 1971-2000. Data collected first day of the month.

Literature Cited

Crozier, L. G., A. P. Hendry, P. W. Lawson, T. P. Quinn, N. J. Mantua, J. Battin, R. G. Shaw, and R. B. Huey. 2008. Potential responses to climate change in organisms with complex life histories: Evolution and plasticity in Pacific salmon. Evolutionary Applications 1(2): 252–270, doi:10.1111/j.1752-4571.2008.00033.x.

Davey, C. A., K. T. Redmond, D. B. Simeral. 2006. Weather and climate inventory National Park Service North Coast and Cascades Network. Natural Resource Technical Report NPS/NCCN/NRTR—2006/010. National Park Service, Fort Collins, Colorado. Available online: https://irma.nps.gov/Reference.mvc/DownloadDigitalFile?code=147109&file=2006_10_23_nccninventory_final.pdf (accessed 6 February 2012).

Gray, S. 2008. Framework for linking climate, resource inventories and ecosystem monitoring. Natural Resource Technical Report NPS/GRYN/NRTR-2008/110. National Park Service, Fort Collins, Colorado.

Hamlet, A. F., P. W. Mote, M. P. Clark, and D. P. Lettenmaier. 2007. 20th century trends in runoff, evapotranspiration, and soil moisture in the Western U.S. Journal of Climate 20(8): 1468-1486. DOI: 10.1175/JCLI4051.1

Littell, J. S., and R. Gwozdz. 2011. Climatic water balance and regional fire years in the Pacific Northwest, USA: Linking regional climate and fire at landscape scales. Chapter 5, pp. 117-139. In McKenzie, D., C.M. Miller, and D.A. Falk (eds.), The Landscape Ecology of Fire, Ecological Studies 213, Springer, Dordrecht, The Netherlands, doi 10.1007/978-94-007-0301-8_5.

Lofgren, R., B. Samora, B. Baccus, and B. Christoe. 2010. Climate monitoring protocol for the North Coast and Cascades Network (Mount Rainier National Park, Olympic National Park, North Cascades National Park, Lewis and Clark National Historical Park, Ebey's Landing National Historical Reserve, San Juan Islands National Historical Park, Fort Vancouver National Historic Site): volume 1. narrative and appendices, version 5/26/2010. Natural Resource Report NPS/NCCN/NRR—2010/240. National Park Service, Fort Collins, Colorado.

Mantua, N. 2010. The Joint Institute for the Study of the Atmosphere and Oceans, University of Washington. *The Pacific Decadal Oscillation* website. http://www.atmos.washington.edu/~mantua/REPORTS/PDO/PDO_egec.htm (accessed 2 November 2011).

Nakawatase, J. M., and D. L. Peterson. 2006. Spatial variability in forest growth – climate relationships in the Olympic Mountains, Washington. Canadian Journal of Forest Resources 36:77–91.

National Weather Service Glossary. National Oceanic and Atmospheric Administration. Website http://weather.gov/glossary/ (accessed 30 March 2011).

Redmond, K. 1998. Western Regional Climate Center, Desert Research Institute. El Niño, La Nina, and the Western U.S., *Alaska and Hawaii Frequently Asked Questions* website. http://www.wrcc.dri.edu/enso/ensofaq.html (accessed 30 March 2011).

Thompson, R., M. Ventura, and L. Camarero. 2009. On the climate and weather of mountain and sub-arctic lakes in Europe and their susceptibility to future climate change. Freshwater Biology 54:2433-2451.

Appendix A: Marblemount (Darrington 21NNE) USCRN - Water Year 2010.

Temperatures ranged from an extreme low of 11.1°F on December 19, 2010 to a high of 98.4°F on August 15 (Table A-1). Data from this site reflects the warmer than average conditions during the months of January and February, and the unusually cool spring and summer (Figure A-1). The months of April through September were below average in temperature, with May the most extreme at 4.2°F below average.

Marblemount received a total of 80 inches of precipitation in Water Year 2010 (Table A-1). The period of late spring through early summer (April, May and June) was much wetter than average (122%, 159% and 151% of normal respectively). September was significantly wetter than normal with 8.1 inches of rain, more than twice the average for the period of record (Figure A-3). July was significantly drier than normal with only 0.1 inches of rain, or 6% of average rainfall (Figures A-3, A-4). Between July 4 and August 2, no precipitation was recorded at this site. The heaviest period of precipitation was November 15 to 26, a total of 10.9 inches of rain (Figure A-5). The daily extreme was November 16, with 2.5 inches of rain (Figure A-5).

Table A-1. Monthly summary data, Marblemount USCRN, Water Year 2010.

Season	Month & Year	Mean Air Temp °F	Max Daily Air Temp °F	Min Daily Air Temp °F	Precipitation (inches)
Fall	October 2009	47.2	66.6	24.6	14.1
	November 2009	41.1	57.7	29.7	17.7
Winter	December 2009	32.4	54.0	11.1	5.5
	January 2010	41.8	57.2	28.4	8.7
	February 2010	42.0	58.6	26.8	3.3
Spring	March 2010	43.1	79.0	27.5	6.4
	April 2010	46.4	80.4	28.6	4.6
	May 2010	50.7	76.1	32.5	5.7
Summer	June 2010	56.4	77.9	39.9	3.3
	July 2010	62.9	94.3	44.1	0.1
	August 2010	62.7	98.4	40.8	2.6
Fall	September 2010	57.5	83.5	40.5	8.1
Water Year Total		**48.7**	**98.4**	**11.1**	**80.0**

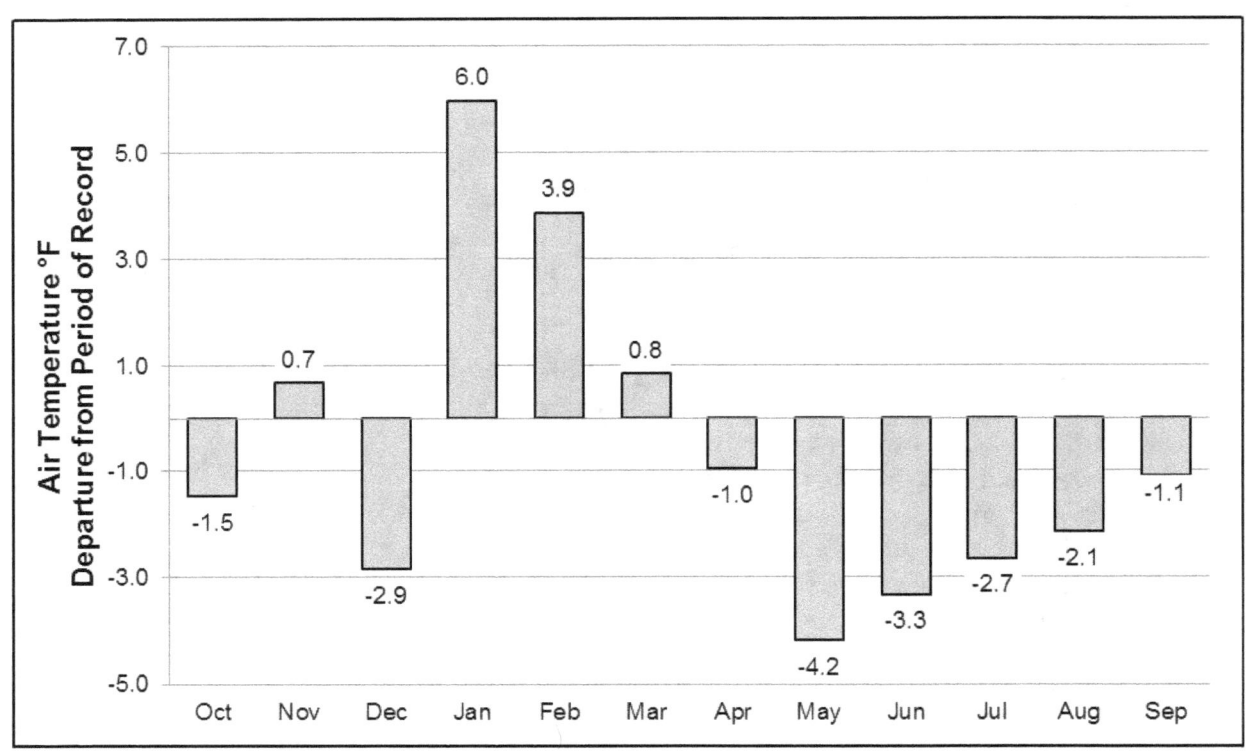

Figure A-1. Comparison of average monthly temperature (°F) at Marblemount USCRN in Water Year 2010 against monthly averages for period of record (2003-2010).

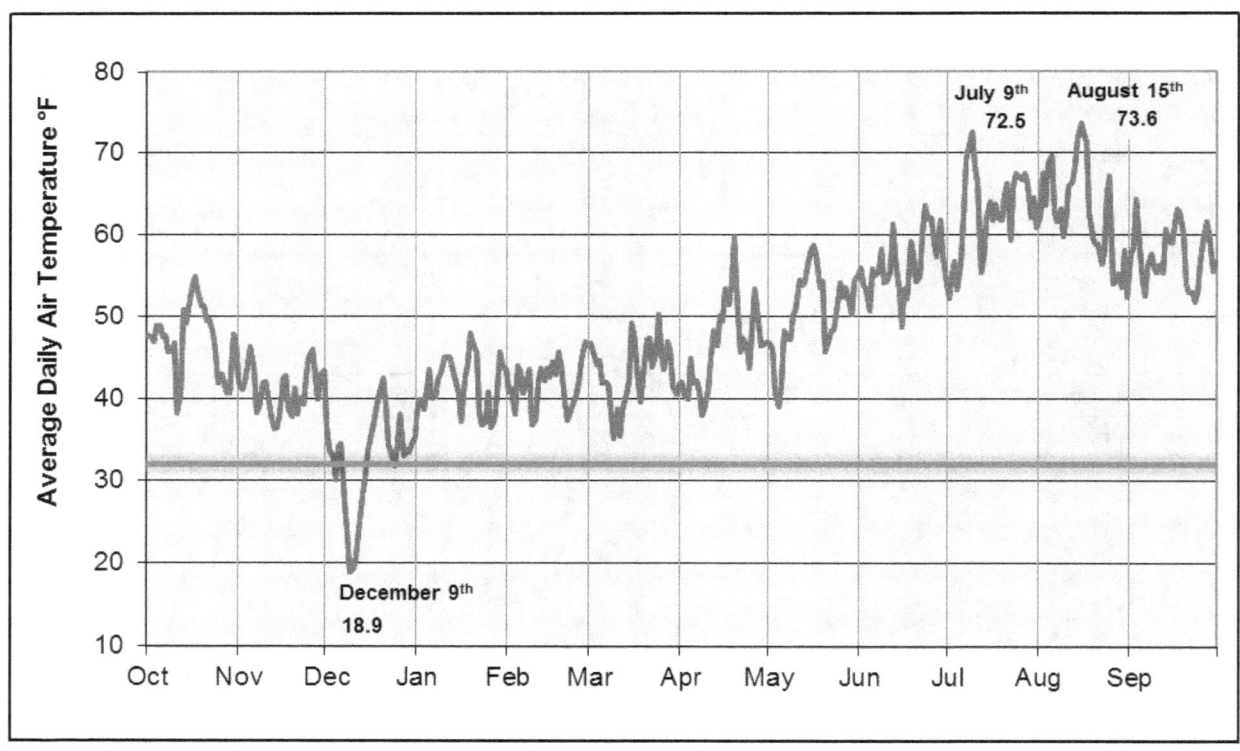

Figure A-2. Daily average air temperature (°F) at Marblemount USCRN, Water Year 2010.

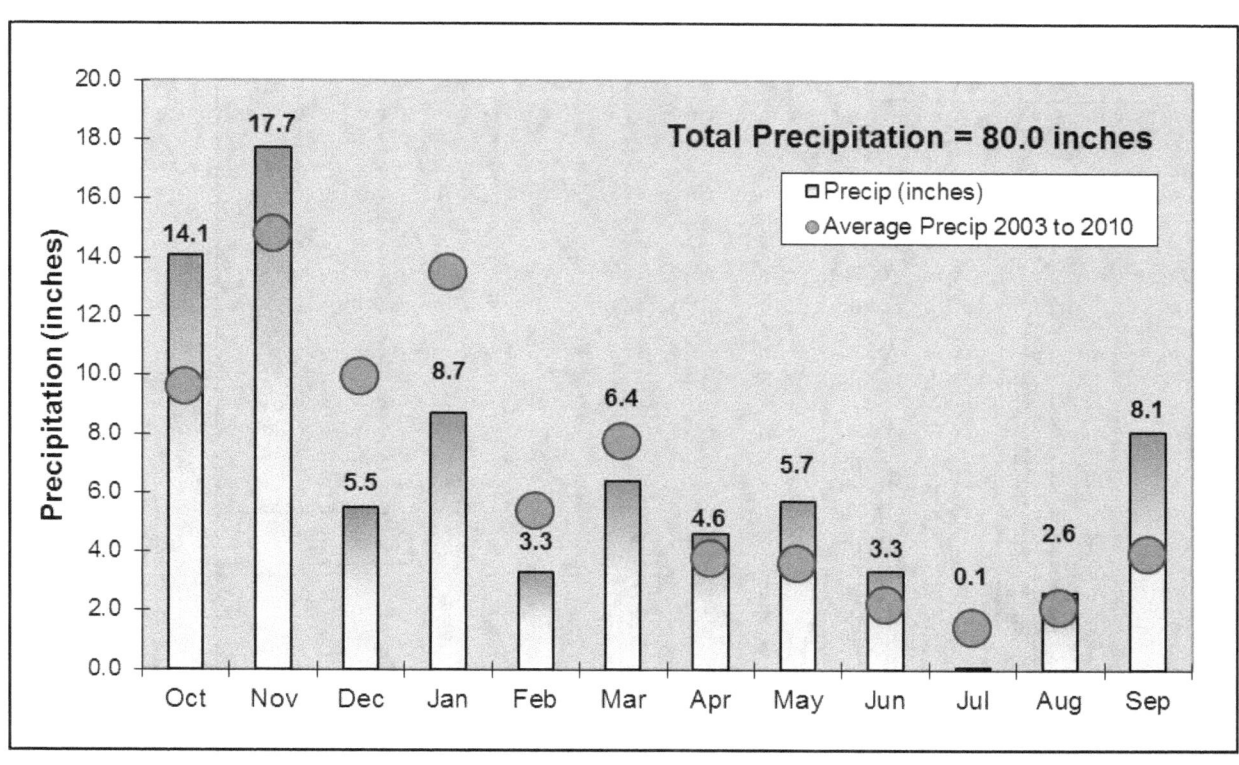

Figure A-3. Monthly precipitation values at Marblemount USCRN, Water Year 2010 compared to the monthly averages for the period of record (2003-2010).

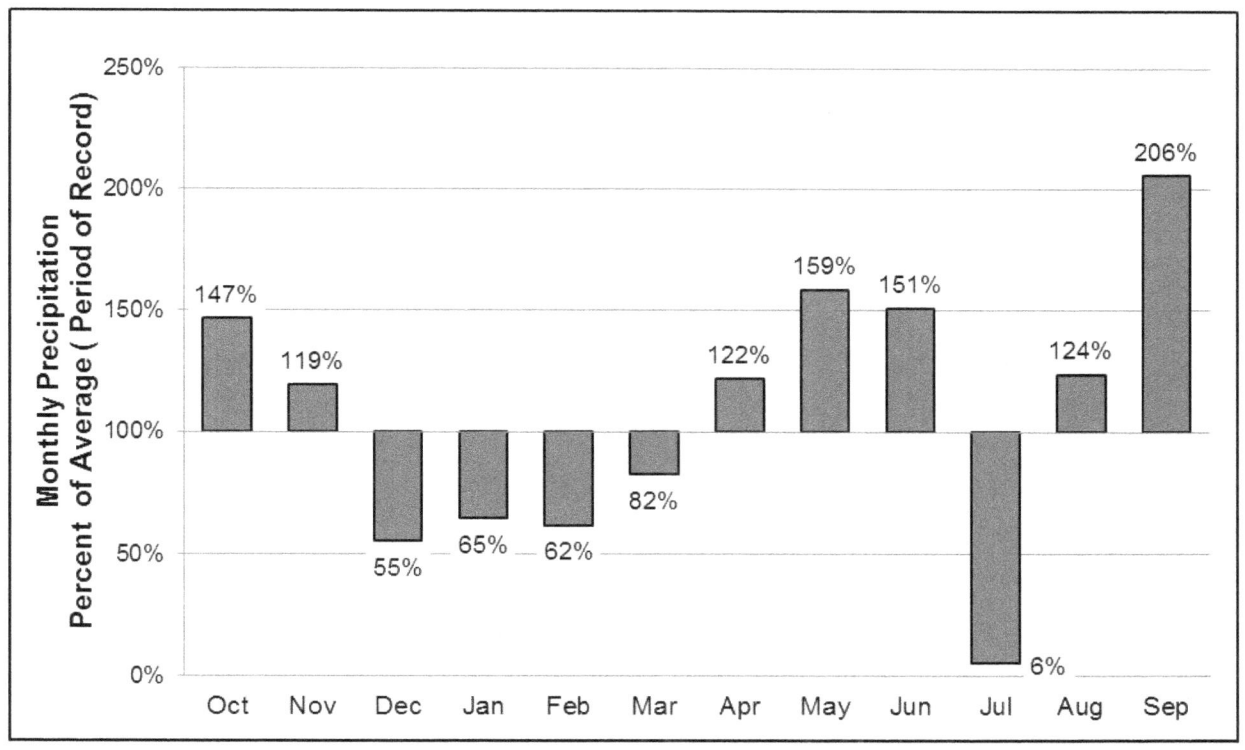

Figure A-4. Percent of average for the period of record (2003-2010) for precipitation at Marblemount USCRN, Water Year 2010.

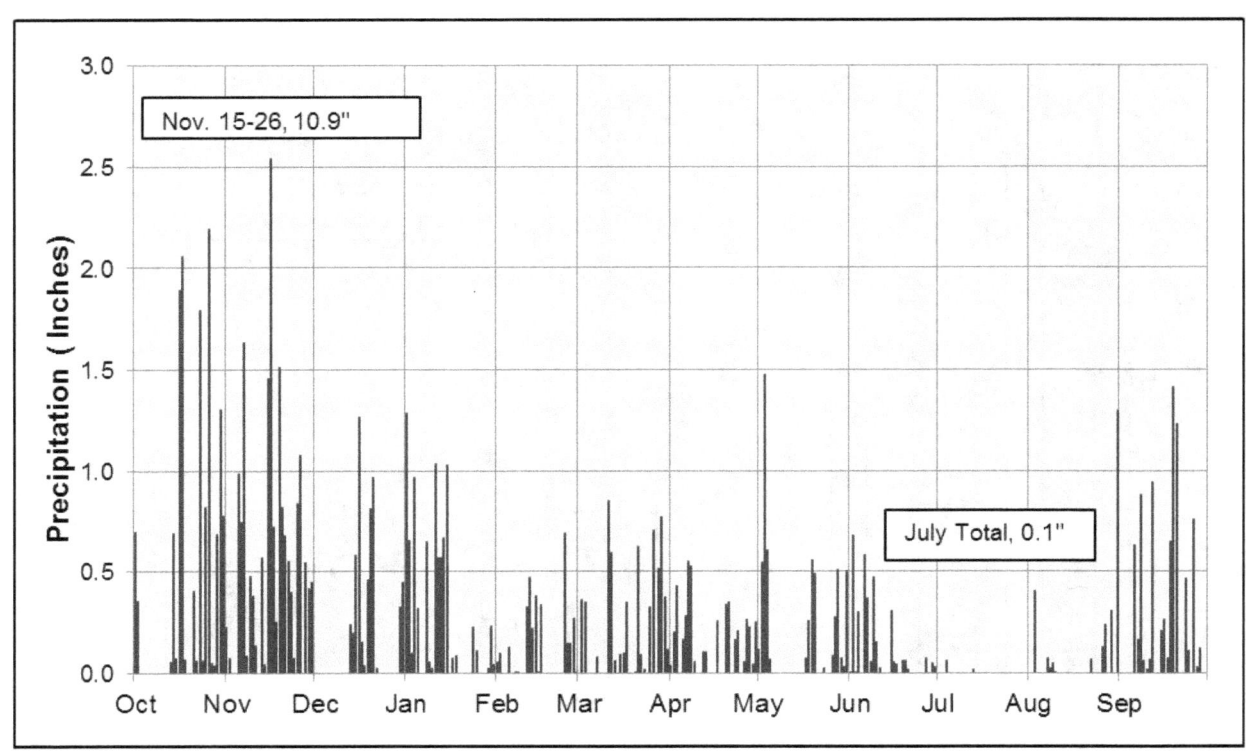

Figure A-5. Daily precipitation (inches) at Marblemount USCRN, Water Year 2010.

Appendix B: Park Creek Ridge SNOTEL - Water Year 2010.

Temperatures ranged from an extreme low of 3.0°F to a high of 80.6°F (Figure B-1). Late fall and early winter months were much colder than average. The largest departure from normal was observed in December with temperature 6.9°F below normal. February was significantly warmer than normal, with a 4.0° F departure from the period of record (Figure B-1). The colder than average temperatures of fall and early winter were replaced by warmer conditions during the months of January, February and March (3.6 above average; Figure B-1). Late spring returned to slightly cooler than average temperatures, especially in the month of May (1.5 below average) (Figure B-1).

The Park Creek Ridge SNOTEL received 65.7 inches of precipitation in Water Year 2010 (Figure B-1). Fall months were wetter than average with October significantly wetter than normal at 9.3 inches of rain, more than four times the average for the period of record (Figures B-3 and B-4). July was significantly drier than normal with only 0.1 inches of rain, 8% of the average rainfall. The months of August and September were both wetter than normal, at 200% and 274% of average, respectively.

Snowpack at Park Creek Ridge remained slightly below normal for most of the winter and spring months. Snowpack began developing on November 5, 2009 and melted out on June 18, 2010, persisting for 225 days (Figure B-6). On April 1, the snowpack was 90% of normal (Figure B-7).

Table B-1. Monthly summary data Park Creek Ridge SNOTEL, Water Year 2010.

Season	Month & Year	Mean Air Temp °F	Max Daily Air Temp °F	Min Daily Air Temp °F	Precipitation (inches)
Fall	October 2009	37.7	54.9	22.1	9.2
	November 2009	31.4	45.0	20.7	15.5
Winter	December 2009	22.4	39.2	3.0	4.5
	January 2010	28.2	41.0	14.9	10.7
	February 2010	31.1	43.9	24.4	4.1
Spring	March 2010	33.5	46.9	18.1	5.1
	April 2010	35.7	59.5	19.4	3.8
	May 2010	40.3	62.6	25.0	3.5
Summer	June 2010	47.4	65.8	33.1	2.7
	July 2010	57.1	79.0	36.7	0.1
	August 2010	57.1	80.6	38.3	2.0
Fall	September 2010	48.5	72.7	37.4	4.5
Water Year Total		**39.2**	**80.6**	**3.0**	**65.7**

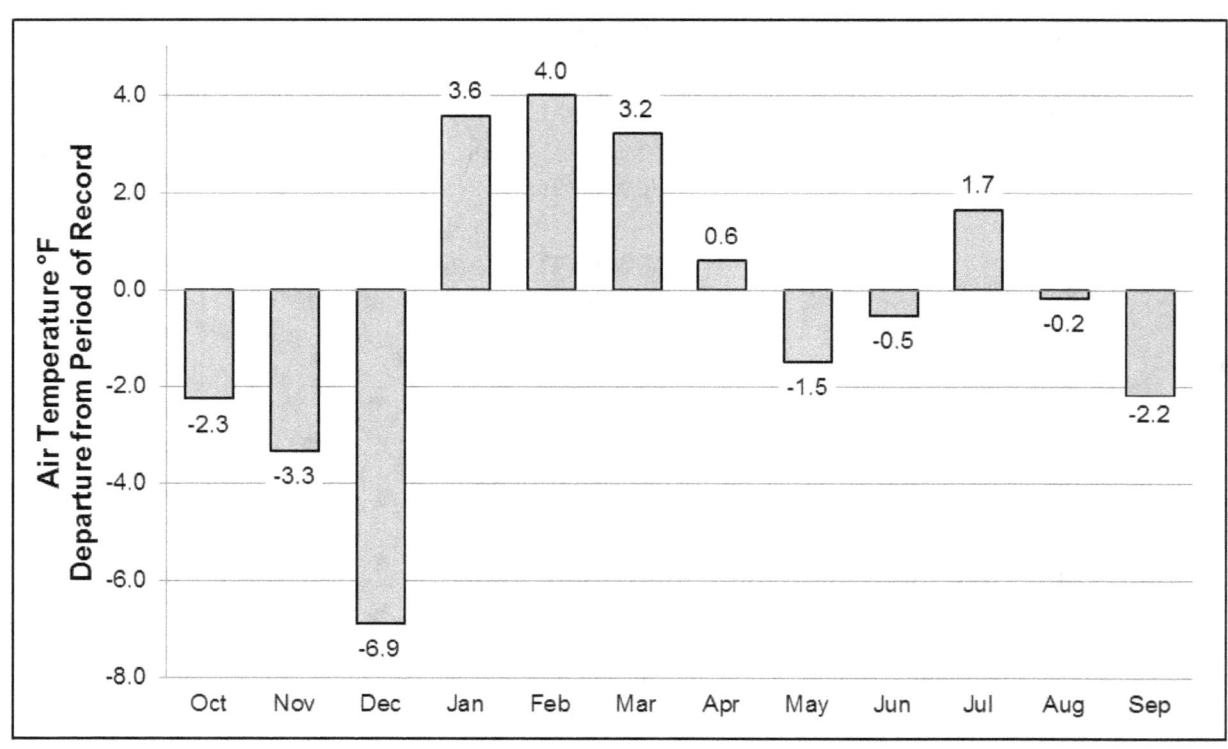

Figure B-1. Comparison of average monthly temperature (°F) for Park Creek Ridge SNOTEL in Water Year 2010 against monthly averages for the period of record (1979-2010).

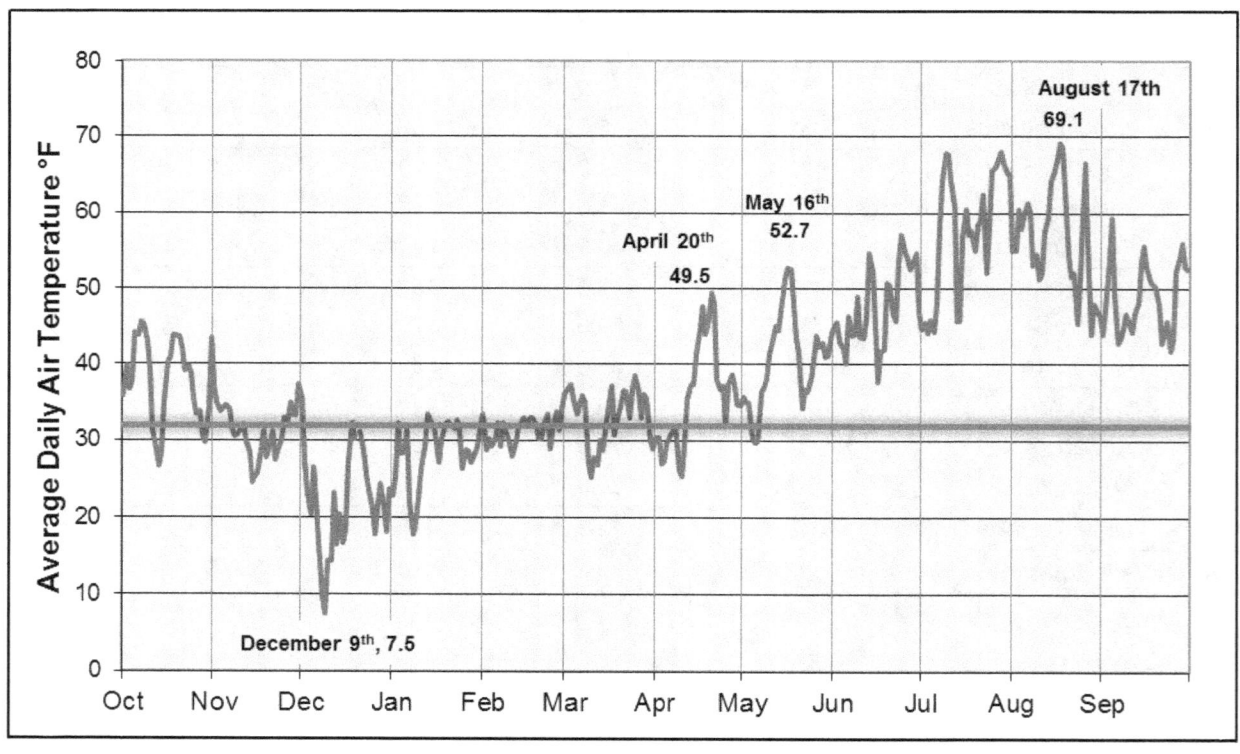

Figure B-2. Daily average air temperature (°F) at Park Creek Ridge SNOTEL, Water Year 2010.

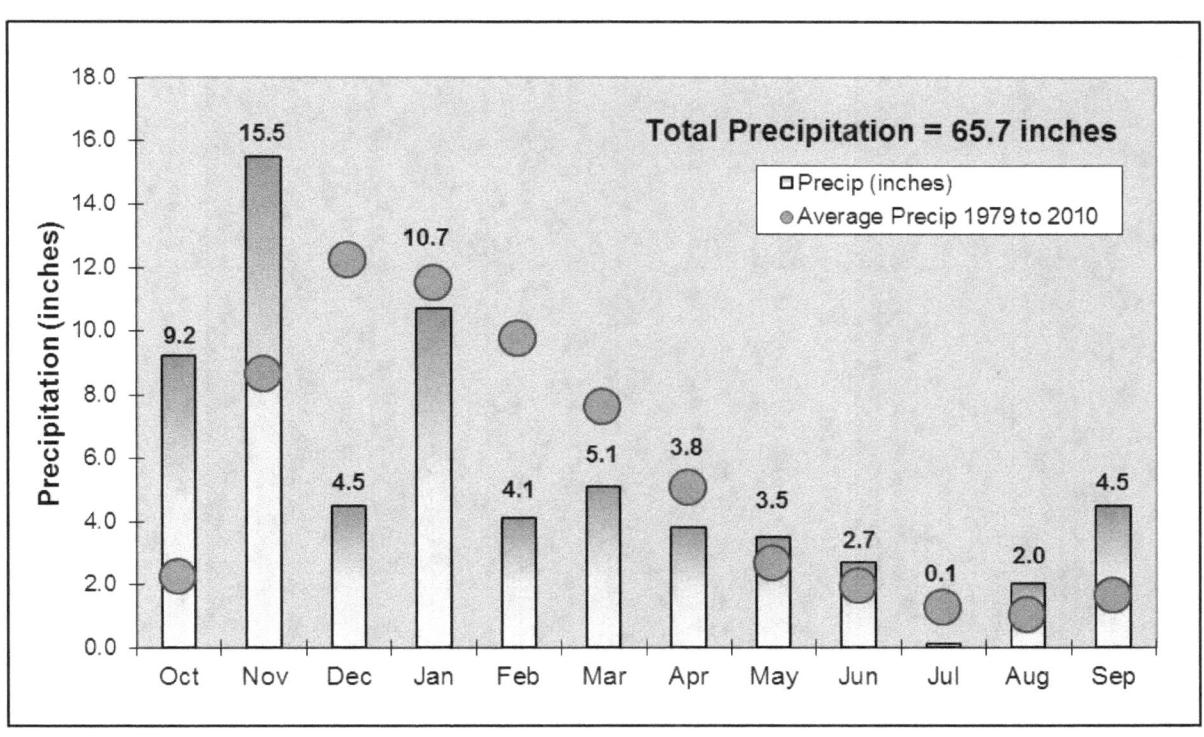

Figure B-3. Monthly precipitation values at Park Creek Ridge SNOTEL, Water Year 2010 compared to the monthly averages for the period of record (1979-2010).

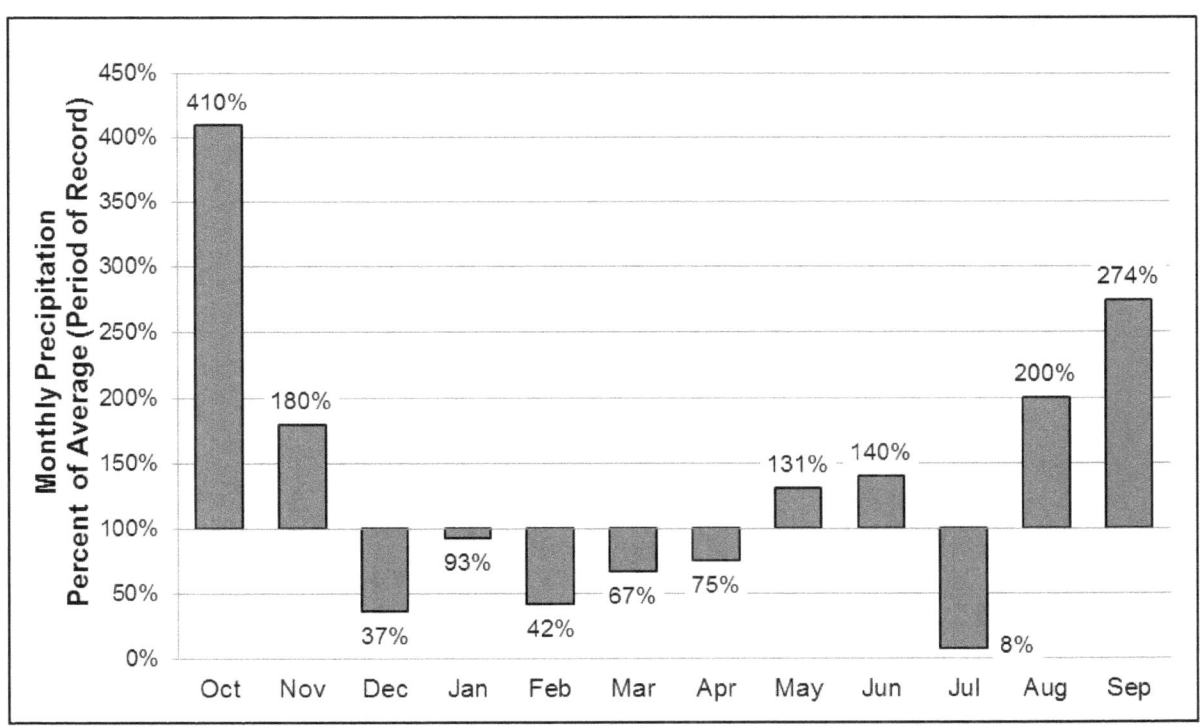

Figure B-4. Percent of average for the period of record (1979-2010) for precipitation at Park Creek Ridge SNOTEL in Water Year 2010.

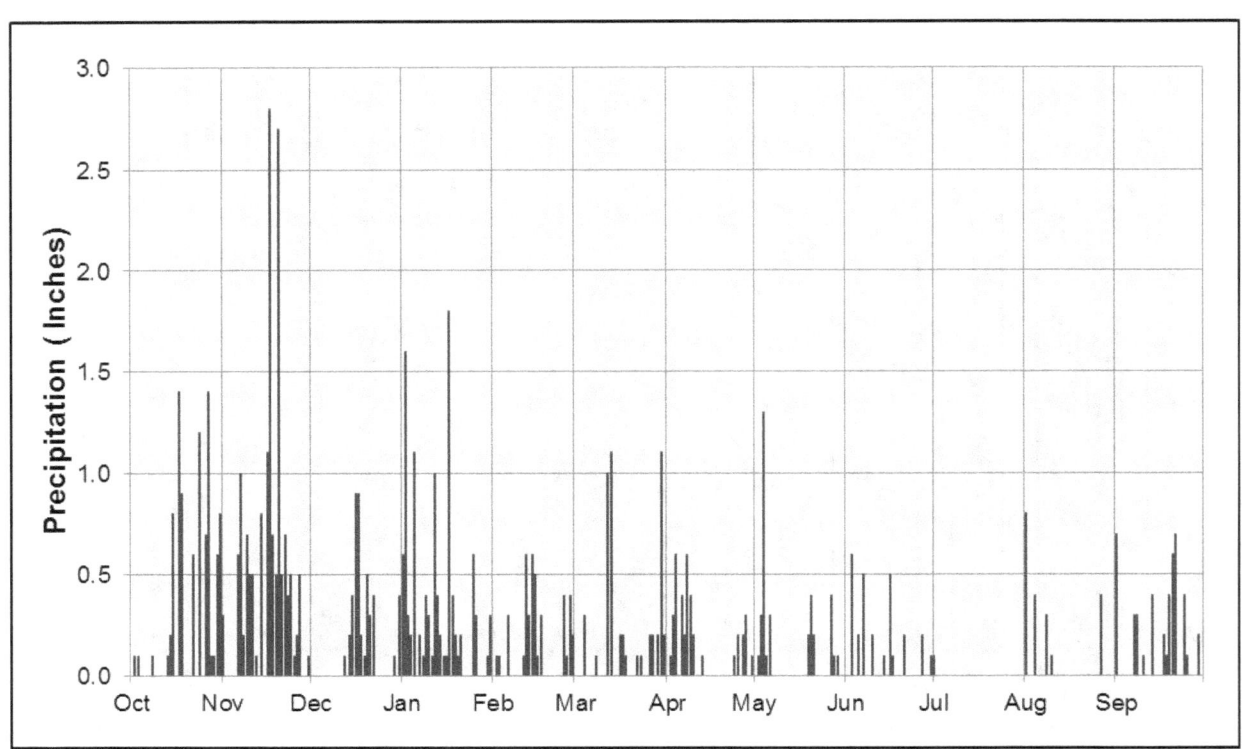

Figure B-5. Daily precipitation (inches) at Park Creek Ridge SNOTEL, Water Year 2010.

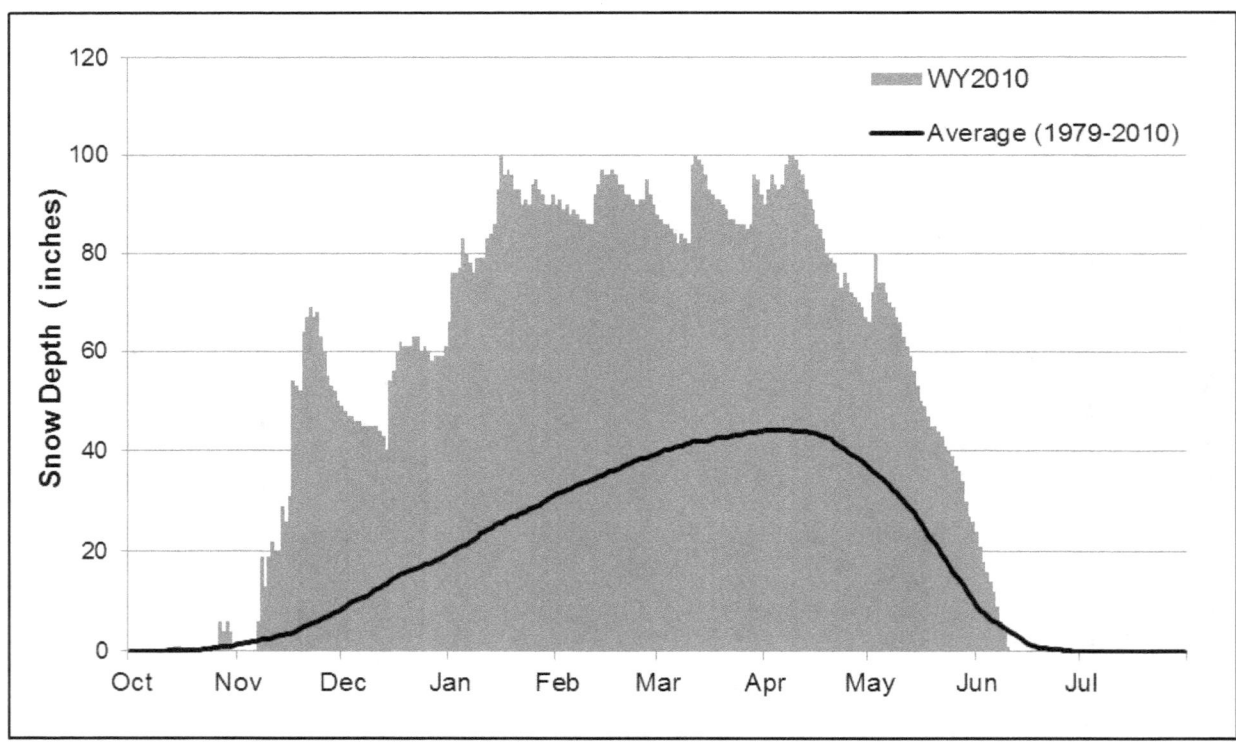

Figure B-6. Daily snow depth (inches) at Park Creek Ridge SNOTEL, Water Year 2010.

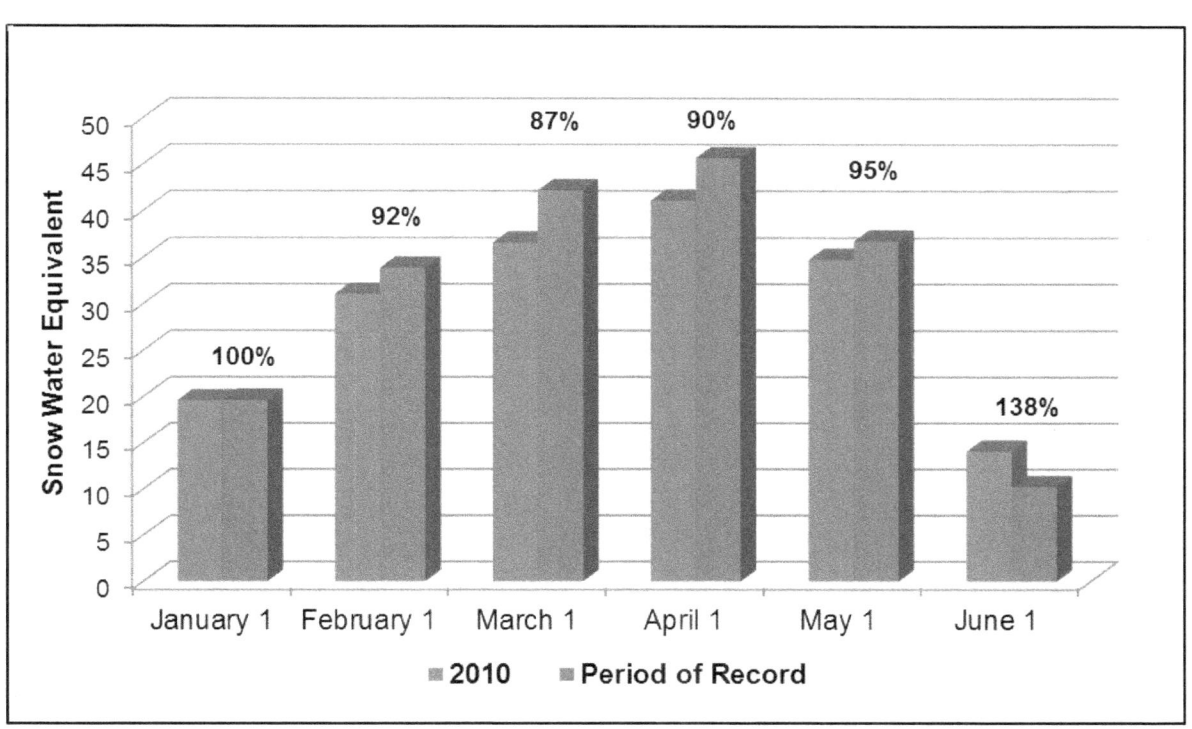

Figure B-7. First of the month snow water equivalent at Park Creek Ridge SNOTEL in Water Year 2010, compared with the period of record (1928-2010).

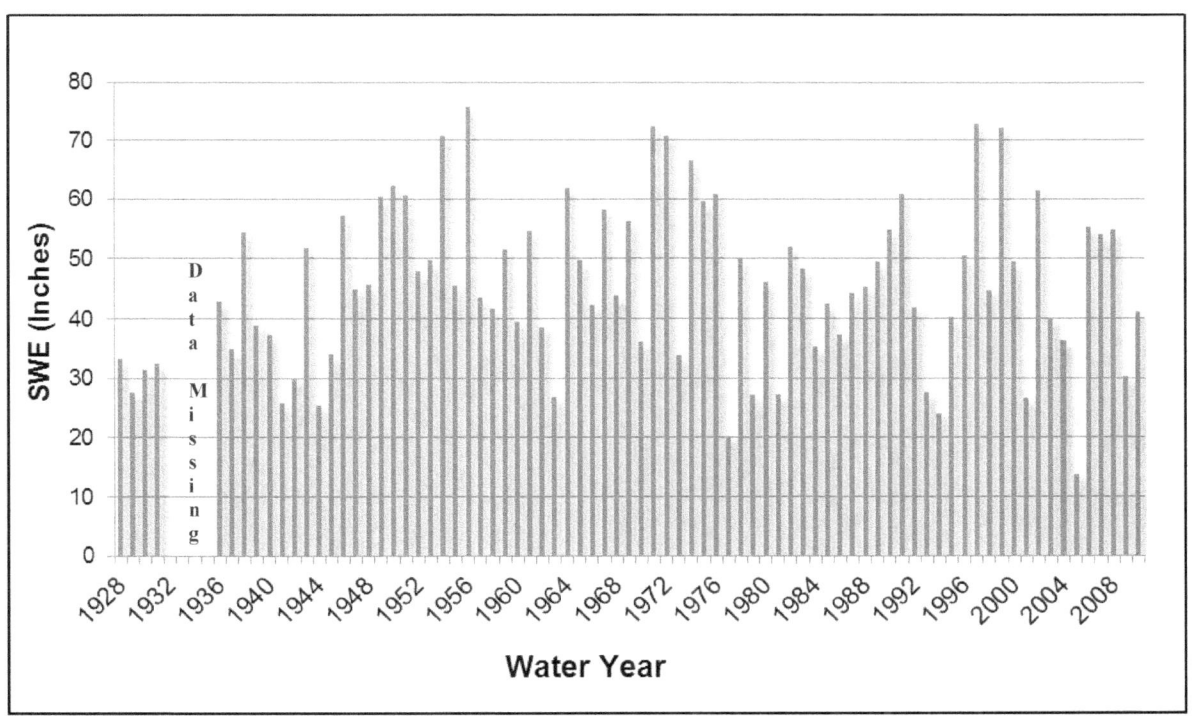

Figure B-8. April 1st snow water equivalent at Park Creek Ridge SNOTEL for the period of record (1928 - 2010). Highlighted column indicates Water 2010. No data were available for water years 1932-1935.

Appendix C: Ross Dam COOP - Water Year 2010.

Temperatures at Ross Dam ranged from an extreme low of 15°F in mid-December 2009 to a high of 95°F in July 2010 (Table C-1). December was significantly cooler than normal with a 2.9°F departure from the period of record. The months of January and February were significantly warmer than average, with a 5.3° and 4.3°F departure from the period of record (Figure C-1). May and June returned to below average temperatures (a departure of -1.0°F for both months) (Figure C-1).

Annual precipitation was 58.5 inches. Winter months were drier than normal. February was significantly drier than normal with only 1.9 inches of rain, 31% percent of the average rainfall in this month (Figures C-3, C-4). Spring and early summer were wetter than normal, with the months of March through June averaging 148% of normal (Figure C-4). September was significantly wetter than normal with 5.7 inches of rain, nearly 2.5 times the average for the period of record (Figures C-3, C-4).

Table C-1. Monthly summary data, Ross Dam COOP, Water Year 2010.

Season	Month & Year	Mean Air Temp °F	Max Daily Air Temp °F	Min Daily Air Temp °F	Precipitation (inches)
Fall	October 2009	48.1	73.0	33.0	9.3
	November 2009	40.0	53.0	31.0	13.9
Winter	December 2009	31.1	46.0	15.0	4.2
	January 2010	38.4	53.0	27.0	6.2
	February 2010	40.7	52.0	29.0	1.9
Spring	March 2010	42.7	63.0	29.0	5.2
	April 2010	45.9	74.0	29.0	3.3
	May 2010	51.7	76.0	34.0	4.3
Summer	June 2010	57.7	80.0	43.0	2.8
	July 2010	66.4	95.0	47.0	0.4
	August 2010	66.2	94.0	47.0	1.4
Fall	September 2010	58.1	85.0	44.0	5.7
Water Year Total		**48.9**	**95.0**	**15.0**	**58.5**

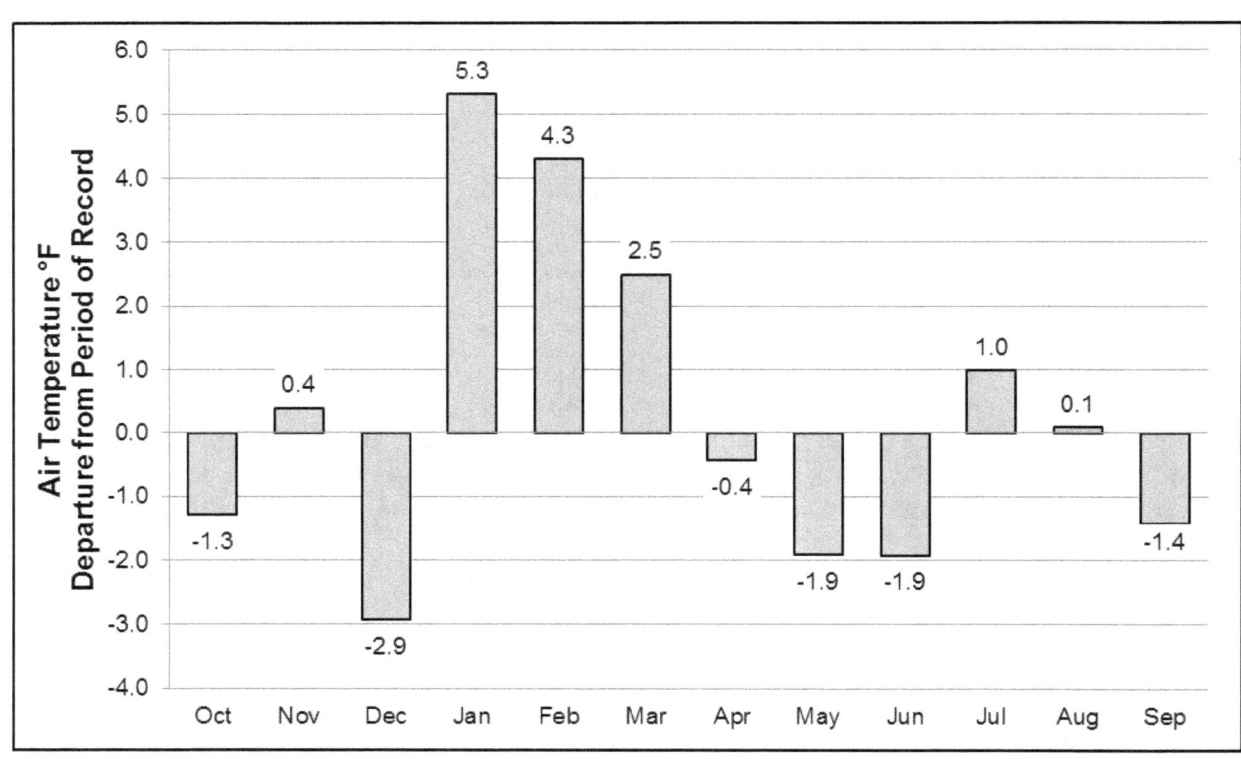

Figure C-1. Comparison of average monthly temperature (°F) for Ross Dam COOP in Water Year 2010 against monthly averages for period of record (1961-2010).

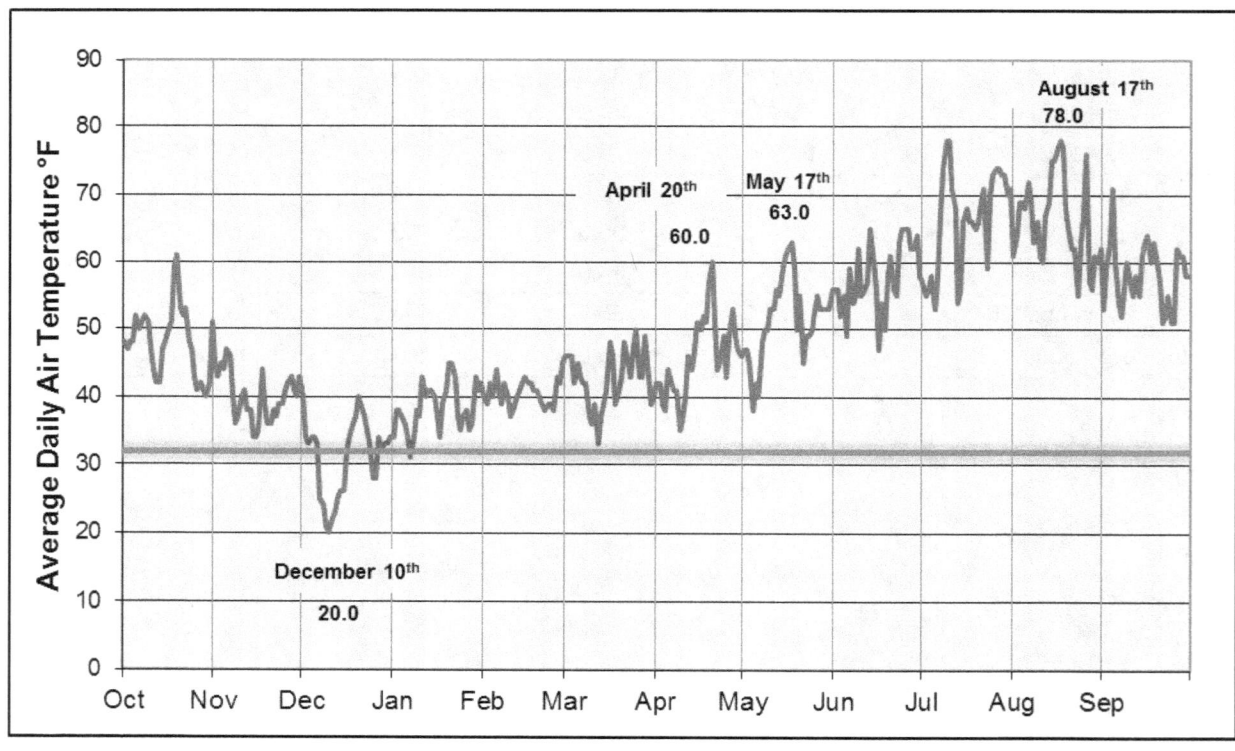

Figure C-2. Daily average air temperature (°F) at Ross Dam COOP, Water Year 2010.

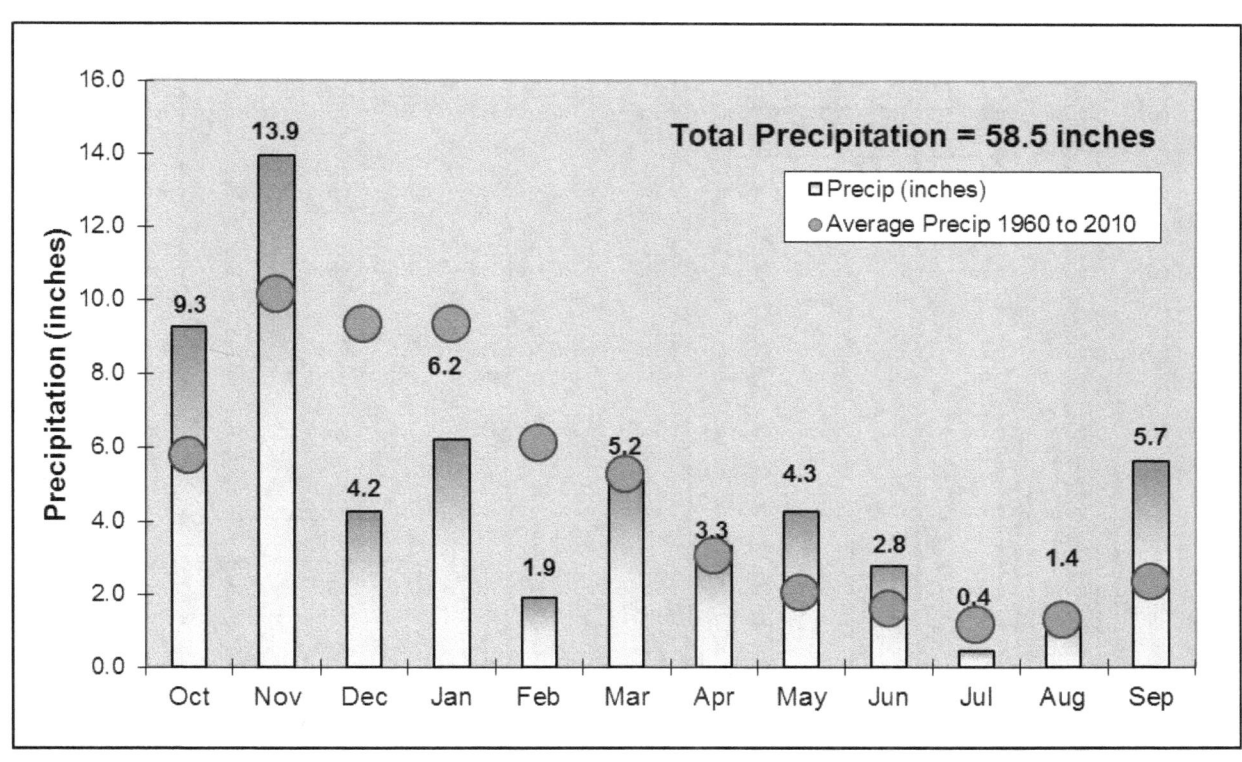

Figure C-3. Monthly precipitation values at Ross Dam COOP, Water Year 2010 compared to the monthly averages for the period of record (1961-2010).

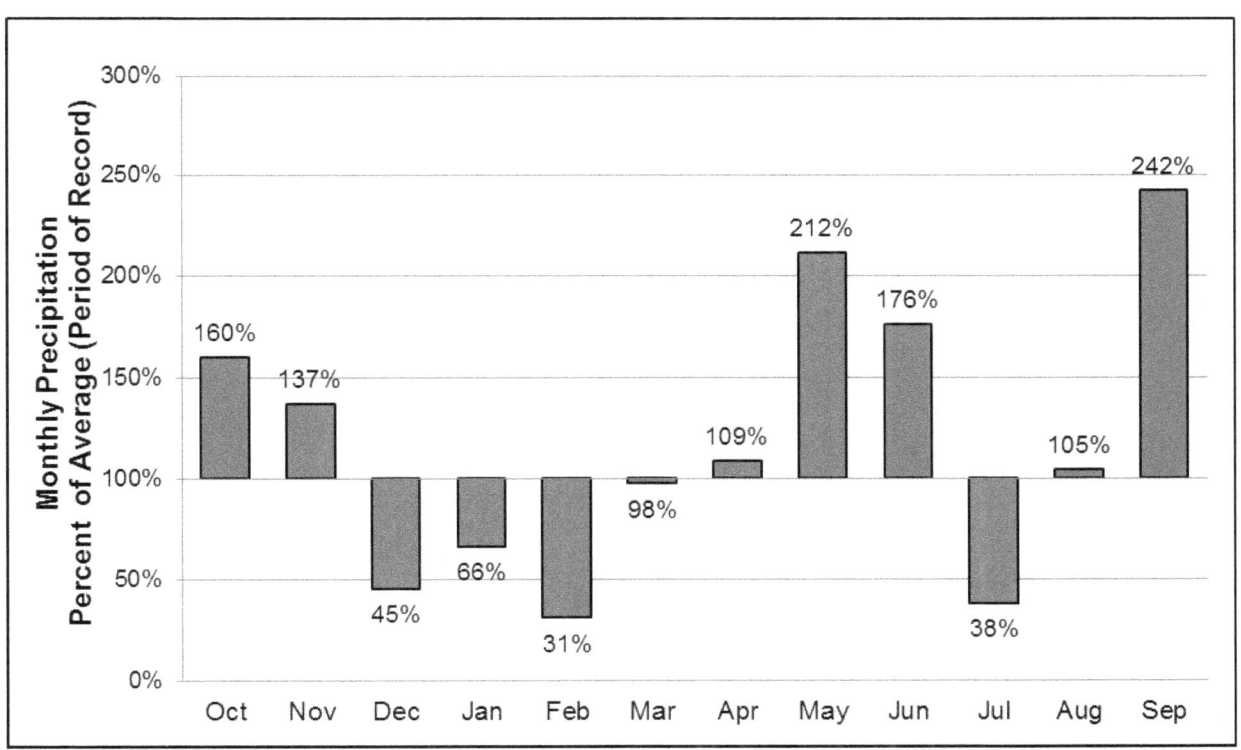

Figure C-4. Percent of average for the period of record (1961-2010) for precipitation at Ross Dam COOP in Water Year 2010.

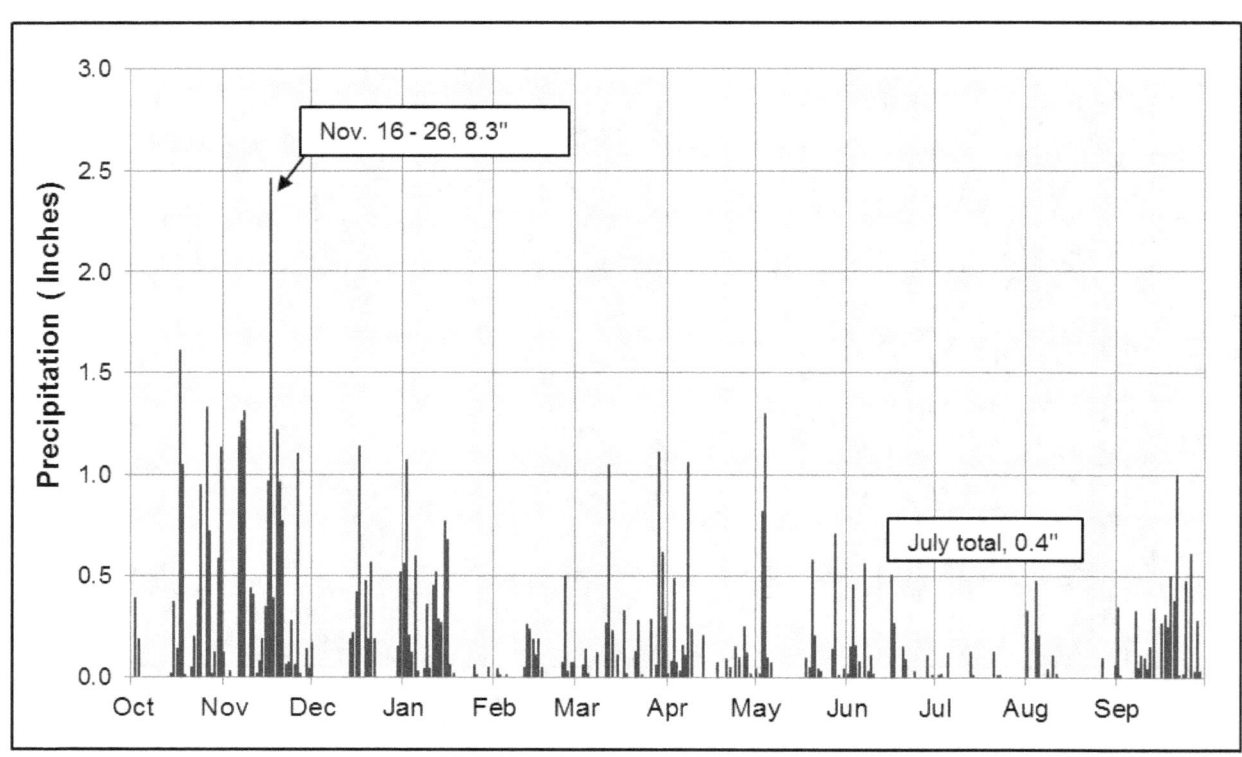

Figure C-5. Daily precipitation (inches) at Ross Dam COOP, Water Year 2010.

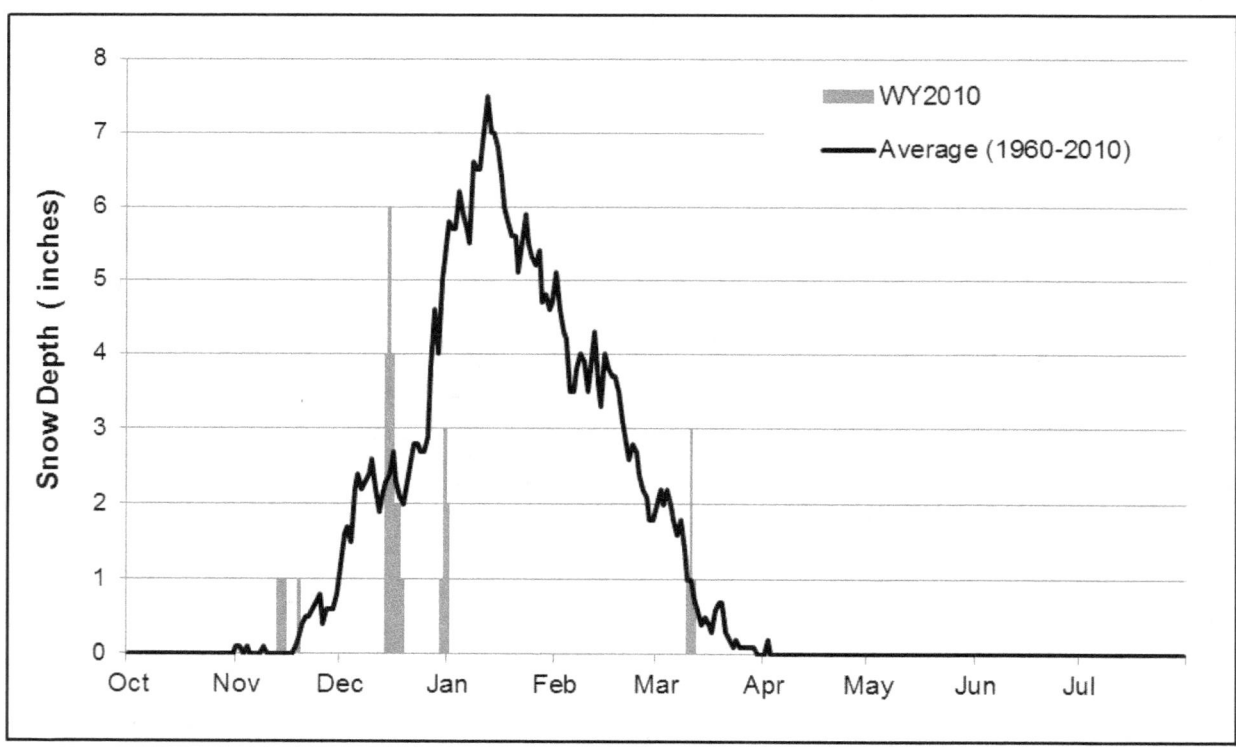

Figure C-6. Daily snow depth (inches) at Ross Dam COOP, Water Year 2010.

Appendix D: Silver Lake GLACIER - Water Year 2010.

Temperatures at Silver Lake ranged from an extreme low of-8.0°F in mid-December 2009 to a high of 76.3°F in July 2010 (Table D-1 and Figure D-1). The Silver Lake GLACIER station was installed in fall 2009. Due to the recent installation of this site, no period of record comparisons can be made.

Table D-1. Monthly summary data, Silver Lake GLACIER, Water Year 2010.

Season	Month & Year	Mean Air Temp °F	Max Daily Air Temp °F	Min Daily Air Temp °F
Fall	October 2009	33.7	50.9	14.9
	November 2009	29.2	50.5	12.0
Winter	December 2009	24.2	48.6	-8.0
	January 2010	31.3	50.7	14.4
	February 2010	29.5	45.7	20.3
Spring	March 2010	29.0	53.6	10.9
	April 2010	30.5	53.6	28.8
	May 2010	36.4	55.8	19.2
Summer	June 2010	43.6	59.0	28.8
	July 2010	55.4	76.3	35.2
	August 2010	53.1	75.0	34.3
Fall	September 2010	45.7	64.8	33.3
Water Year Total		36.8	57.0	20.3

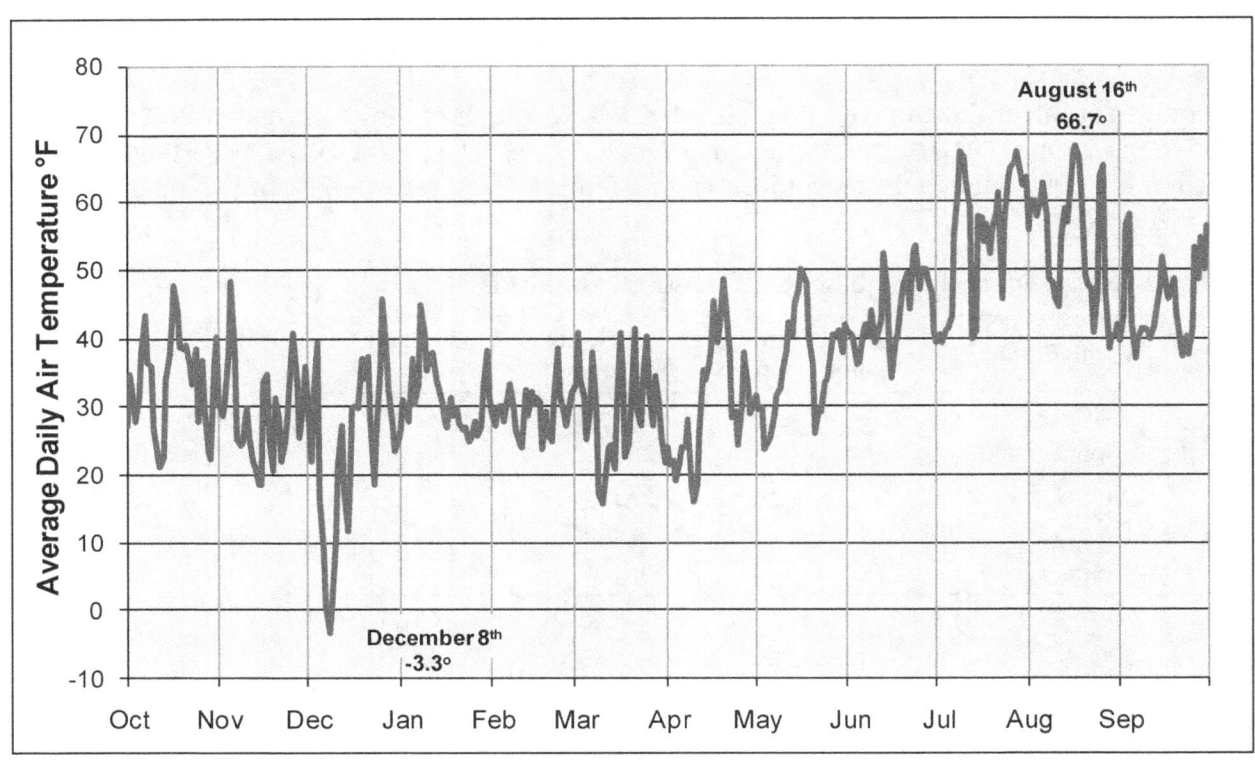

Figure D-1. Daily average air temperature (°F) at Silver Lake GLACIER, Water Year 2010.

Appendix E: Stehekin COOP - Water Year 2010.

Temperatures at Stehekin ranged from an extreme low of 2.3° F on December 9, 2009 to a high of 97° F on July 10, 2010 (Table E-1). December was much colder than average with a departure of -4.2° F (Figure E-1). The months of January, February and March were well above average with departures of +3.7°, +3.0° and +2.6° F. April was slightly cooler than average (-0.8° F) with May even more significantly at 2.5° F below the average. The late summer months of July and August were above average (+2.8° and +1.4° F).

Annual precipitation at Stehekin totaled 3.3 inches. The months of April, May and June were significantly wetter than average. In May, Stehekin received 2.0 inches of rain, more than twice the average for the period of record (Figures E-3, E-4). July was significantly drier than normal with less than 0.1 inches of rain, or eight percent of average rainfall (Figures E-3, E-4).

The Stehekin COOP station is missing all data for September 2010. The source of the missing data is unknown. For this report, missing temperature and precipitation data for the Stehekin COOP has been replaced with data from the nearby Stehekin RAWS station.

Table E-1. Monthly summary data, Stehekin COOP, Water Year 2010.

Season	Month & Year	Mean Air Temp °F	Max Daily Air Temp °F	Min Daily Air Temp °F	Precipitation (inches)
Fall	October 2009	45.1	74.0	23.0	5.9
	November 2009	36.8	55.0	22.0	7.0
Winter	December 2009	25.8	48.0	8.0	2.3
	January 2010	32.2	44.0	14.0	6.5
	February 2010	35.1	47.0	24.0	1.8
Spring	March 2010	41.1	57.0	27.0	1.8
	April 2010	46.5	72.0	26.0	2.5
	May 2010	52.9	81.0	32.0	2.0
Summer	June 2010	61.4	85.0	40.0	1.2
	July 2010	70.6	97.0	48.0	0.0
	August 2010	68.3	95.0	43.0	0.2
Fall	September 2010	58.2[a]	84.0[a]	38.0[a]	1.72[a]
Water Year Total		**46.9**	**97.0**	**8.0**	**31.3**

[a]. The Stehekin COOP station is missing all data for September 2010. For this report, missing temperature and precipitation data for the Stehekin COOP has been replaced with data from the nearby Stehekin RAWS station.

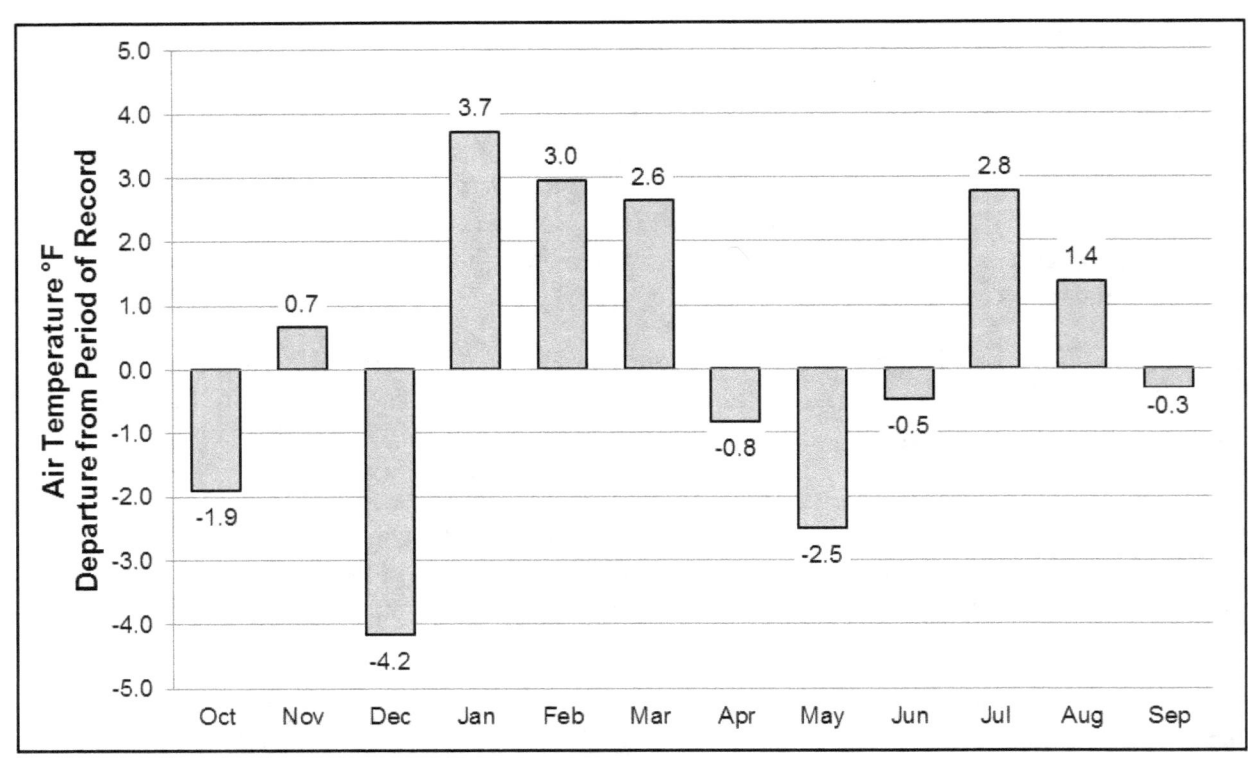

Figure E-1. Comparison of average monthly temperature (°F) for Stehekin COOP in Water Year 2010 against monthly averages for period of record (2003-2010).

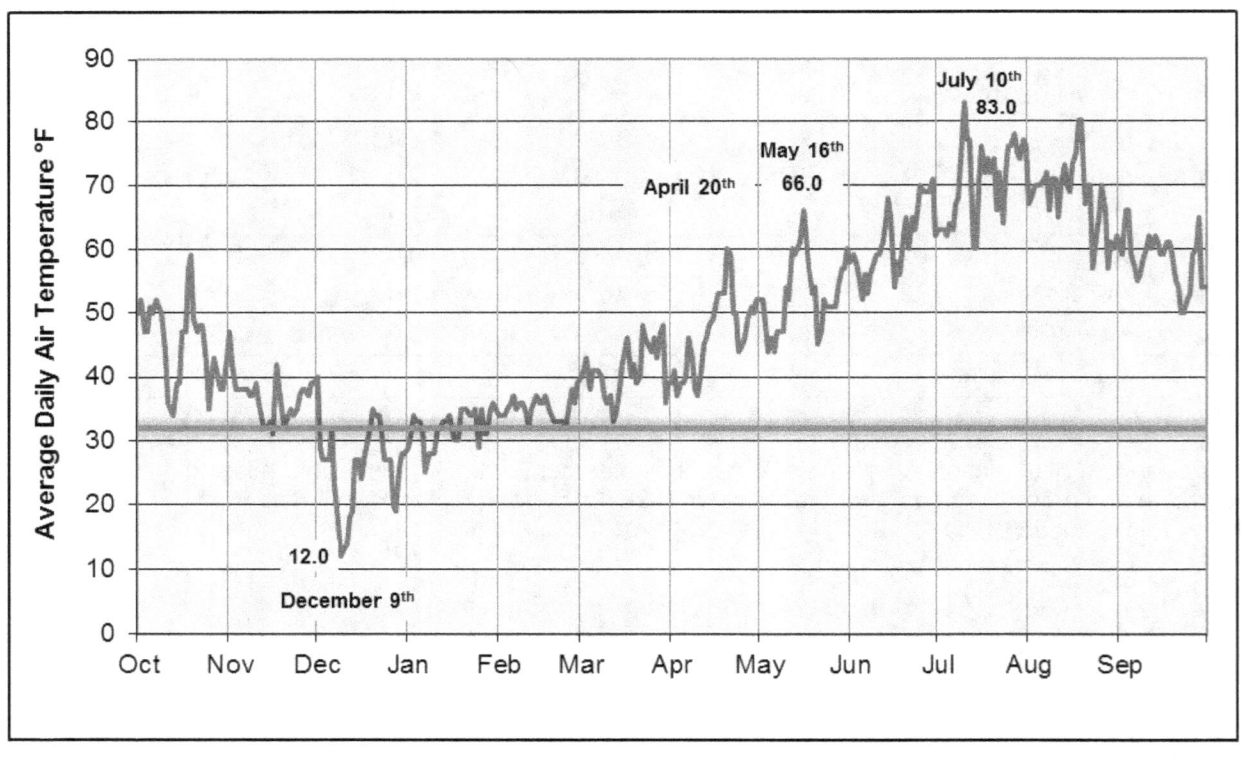

Figure E-2. Daily average air temperature (°F) at Stehekin COOP, Water Year 2010.

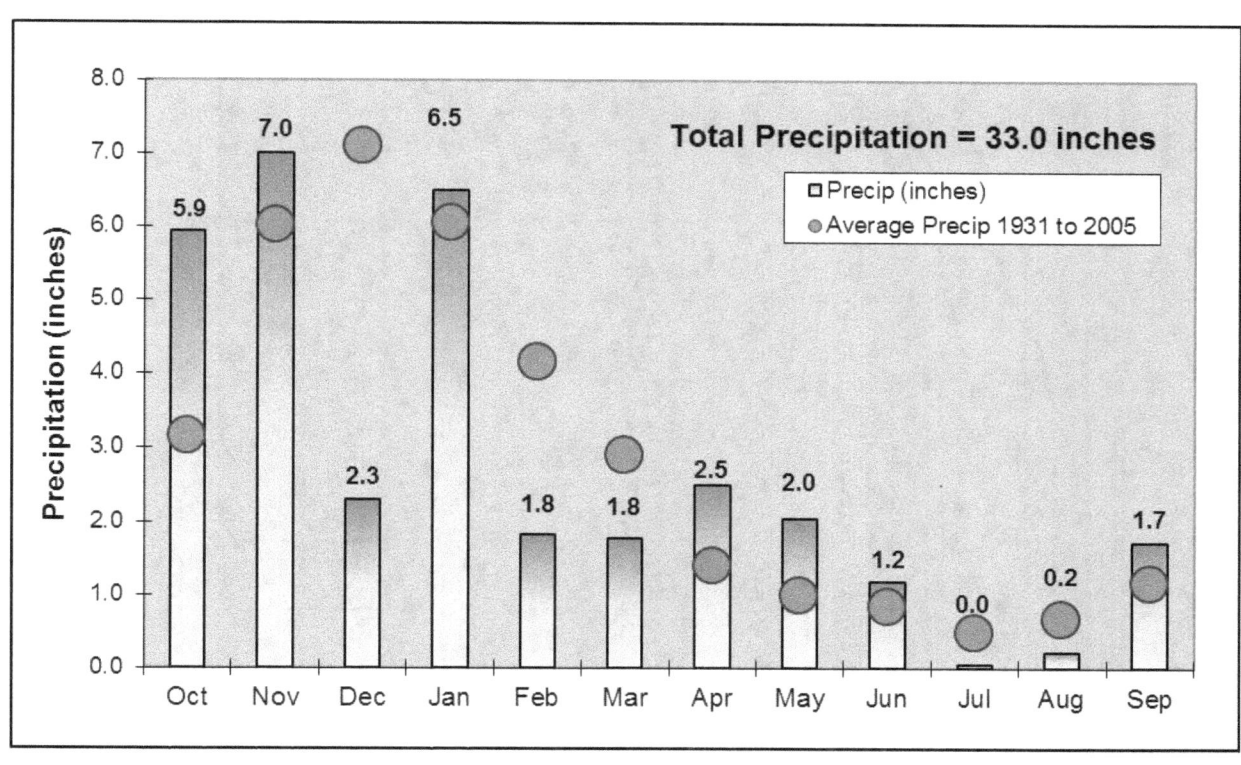

Figure E-3. Monthly precipitation values at Stehekin COOP, Water Year 2010 compared to the monthly averages for the period of record (2003-2010).

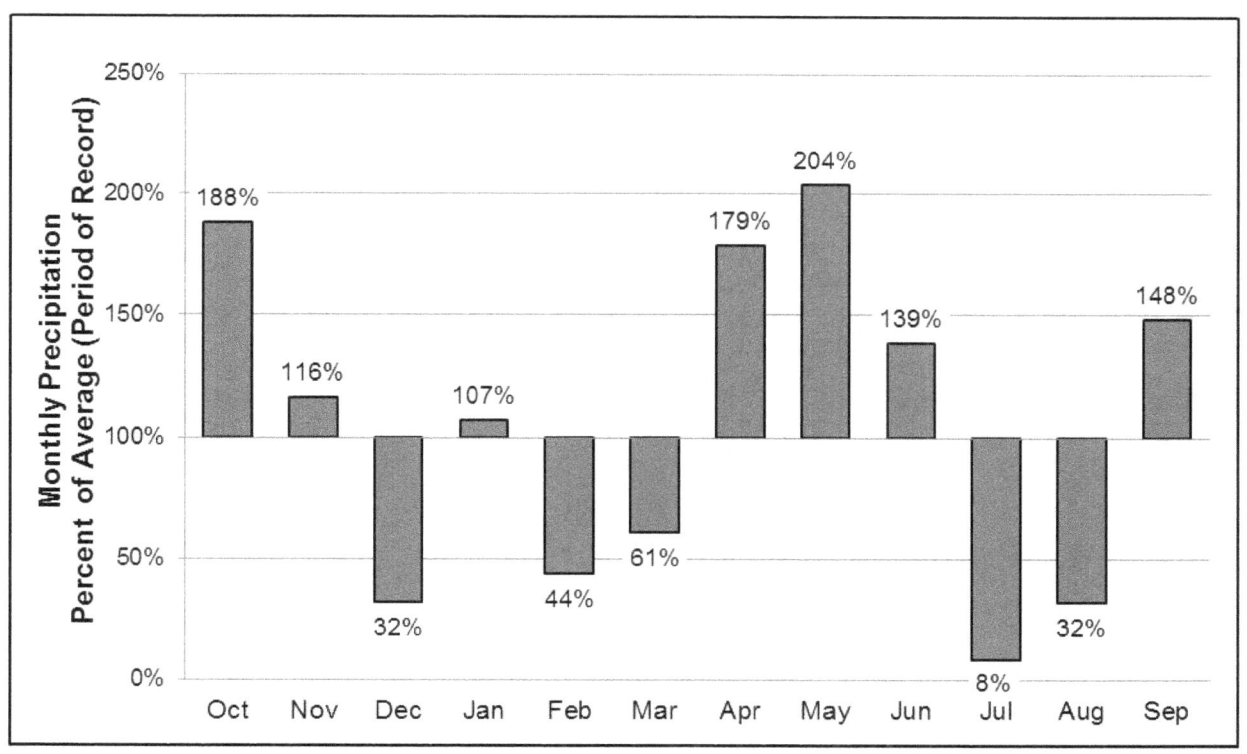

Figure E-4. Percent of average for the period of record (2003-2010) for precipitation at Stehekin COOP, Water Year 2010.

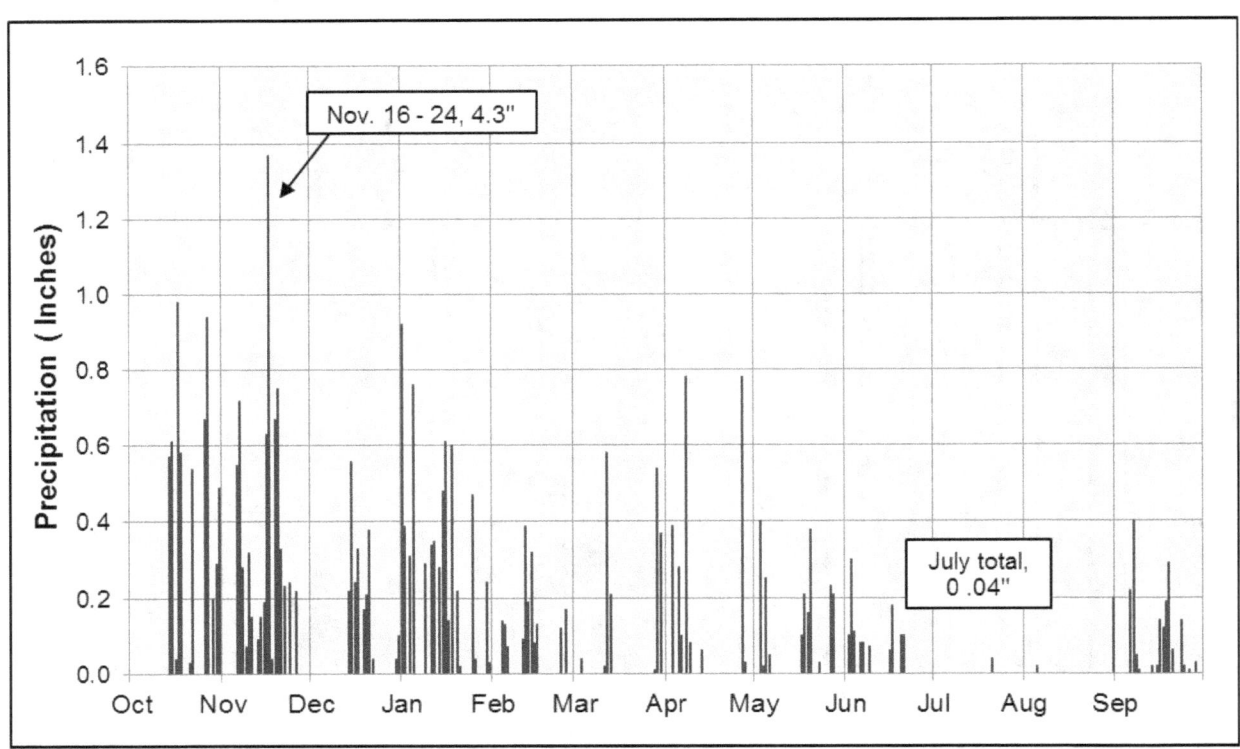

Figure E-5. Daily precipitation (inches) at Stehekin COOP, Water Year 2010.

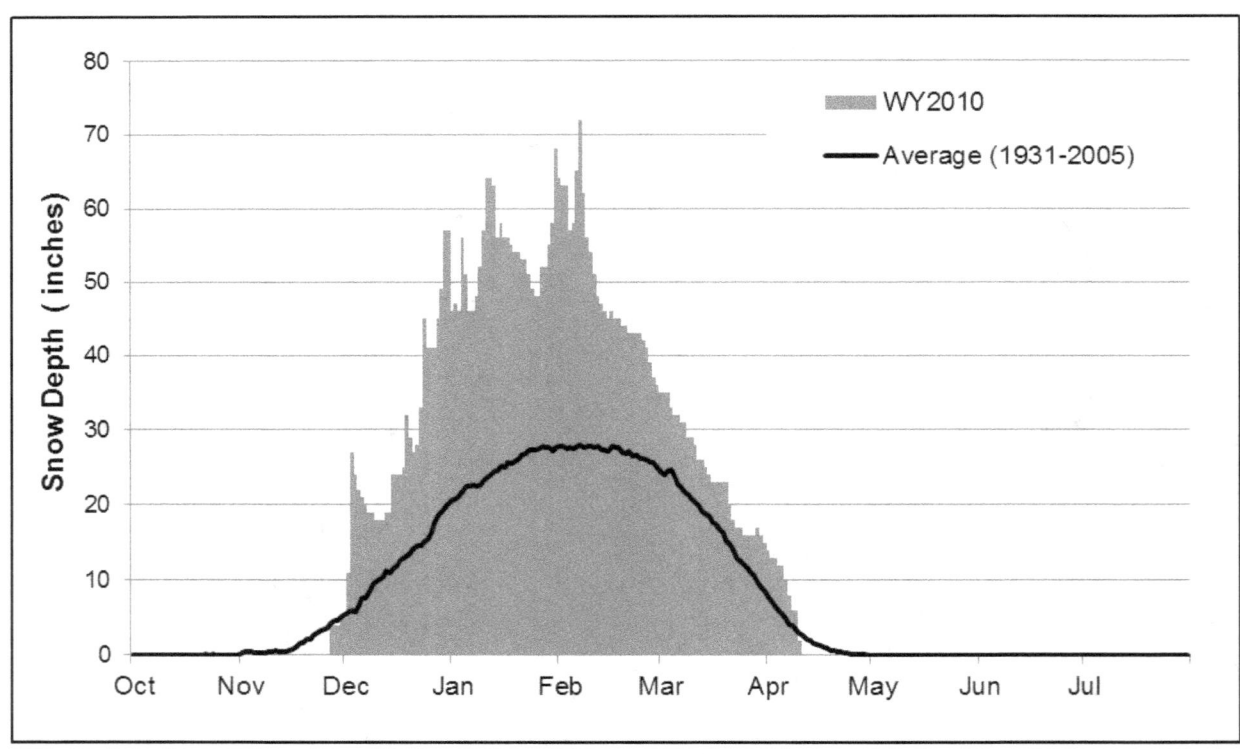

Figure E-6. Daily snow depth (inches) at Stehekin COOP, Water Year 2010.

36